AD • NELL K. DUKE • ANNIE M. MOSES

D0129589

2nd Edition

Beyond Bedtime Stories

A **PARENT'S GUIDE** to
Promoting Reading, Writing, and
Other Literacy Skills From Birth to 5

■SCHOLASTIC

New York • Toronto • London • Auckland • Sydney
Mexico City • New Delhi • Hong Kong • Buenos Aires

Dedications

For all the parents who have generously entrusted me with their children, hopes, and worries through the years. And for the one parent who started it all. Thank you, Mom.

—VSBA

For Mom.

—NKD

For Noah.

—AMM

CREDITS

Pages 13 and 14: From *Language Stories & Literacy Lessons* by Jerome C. Harste, Virginia A. Woodward, and Carolyn L. Burke. Copyright © 1984 by Jerome C. Harste, Virginia A. Woodward, and Carolyn L. Burke. Published by Heinemann, a division of Reed Elsevier, Inc., Portsmouth, NH. All rights reserved.

Page 17: From *Come Along, Daisy!* by Jane Simmons. Copyright © 1997 by Jane Simmons. Used by permission of Little, Brown and Co.

Page 17: From *Madeline* by Ludwig Bemelmans. Copyright © 1939 by Ludwig Bemelmans, renewed © 1967 by Madeleine Bemelmans and Barbara Bemelmans Marciano. Used by permission of Viking Penguin, A Division of Penguin Young Readers Group, A Member of Penguin Group (USA) Inc., New York, NY 10014. All rights reserved.

Page 19: Excerpts from *Starting Out Right: A Guide to Promoting Children's Reading Success.* Copyright © 1999 by the National Academy of Sciences. Reprinted by permission of the National Academies Press, Washington, DC.

Page 61: © book cover and pages extracted from 1998 Scholastic Book Club's product ISBN: 0-590-76962-6.

Page 81: From *On Reading Books to Children* by Van Kleeck/Stahl/Bauer. Copyright © 2003 by Lawrence J. Erlbaum Associates. Reprinted by permission of the publisher.

Page 114: From *Six Sick Sheep: 101 Tongue Twisters* by Joanna Cole and Stephanie Calmenson. Text copyright © 1993 by Joanna Cole and Stephanie Calmenson.

Page 196: From *Alphabet City* by Stephen T. Johnson. Copyright © 1995 by Stephen T. Johnson. Used by permission of Viking Kestrel, A Division of Penguin Young Readers Group, A Member of Penguin Group (USA) Inc., 345 Hudson Street, New York, NY 10014. All rights reserved.

Every effort has been made to find the authors and publishers of previously published material in this book and to obtain permission to print it.

Editor: Raymond Coutu/Lynne Wilson
Cover and interior designer: Maria Lilja/Michelle Kim
Copyeditor: Carol Ghiglieri/Ilise Weiner
Cover photos: Raymond Coutu, Michael Kozura, and Photodisc
ISBN: 978-0-545-65530-9
Copyright © 2013 by V. Susan Bennett-Armistead, Nell K. Duke, and Annie M. Moses

1 2 3 4 5 6 7 8 9 10   23   19 18 17 16 15 14

Contents

Foreword

When my editor approached me to write the foreword to this book, I wondered if I was the best choice. After all, I have no background in child psychology. I have never been a teacher. I'm no "literacy expert." So what was my editor thinking? Then I realized, I do have experience in parenting and, like you, I cared deeply about nurturing the emerging literacy skills of my children, Emily Elizabeth and Timothy, when they were young. I wish this book had been available then. It would have been very helpful.

My wife, Norma, and I were determined to make reading a vital part of Emily's and Tim's lives from birth. For Norma that was important largely because of literacy-related difficulties she experienced as a child. She is dyslexic and suffered, trying to keep up with her classmates during reading time at school.

I was more fortunate. My mother and older brother read to me and with me, and kept me supplied with books. Their efforts paid off; I started reading at an early age, which, I'm confident, gave me a leg-up in reading when I entered school.

So, in 1961 when Emily was born, Norma and I vowed that we would foster a love of reading and books in our children. We supplied Emily and Tim with lots of books and encouraged them to spend lots of time with them. Emily loved books about fairies, wild animals, and pioneer girls. Tim preferred ones about anatomy, dinosaurs, and volcanoes. Reading together was a pleasure, not a chore. Our family loved snuggling up and sharing books. Luckily, we had very poor television reception, so we didn't need to worry too much about that distraction.

Our efforts have paid off. Emily now has a daughter of her own, Alissa. She has been reading to Alissa every day, from the time she was only a couple of months old. She takes writing courses and enjoys writing stories for preteens. Tim and his wife, Tsuyu, live in Paris with their two children, to whom they read in English, French, and, Tsuyu's native language, Japanese. In high school, Tim wrote prize-winning stories and critiques of poetry. Now he writes screenplays.

Although nurturing our children's literacy was a pleasure, it was not always easy. As I said, I wish *Beyond Bedtime Stories* had been available back then to help. One of the things I like most about the book is the information it gives about using storytelling to improve children's reading skills. Norma and I told lots of stories to Emily and Tim when they were growing up, and I continue to tell them to Alissa, who is a tough audience, for sure. Not all that long ago I was telling Alissa a story about a mouse and a princess. I gave the mouse a goofy voice—a voice that, I thought, my little listener would find funny. But instead she placed her hand over my mouth and said, "Not like that. Make him sweet and gentlemanly." Storytelling is a good way to stir a child's imagination—and your own as well.

I also like the fact that Bennett-Armistead, Duke, and Moses discourage us from making reading a competition among children. You'll find no "Billy can read this. Why can't you?" in this book. The authors want reading to be a fun activity and not an SAT test for tots.

I used to visit schools before my age made it difficult. Often, I was asked to judge children's art or writing, which I dreaded because, as a child, my art and writing were not judged well. My pictures were never hung on the wall. My stories were never read to the class. So as an adult, when I would visit schools, I would share my history, praise the work of *all* the children, and tell them, "If somebody doesn't like your picture or story today, he or she may love what you do tomorrow." This is precisely what Bennett-Armistead, Duke, and Moses do here—they urge us to celebrate our children's accomplishments, regardless of how small they may be, in hope of a better tomorrow.

Let's hope that you, the reader, will use the ideas in this book to inspire your little ones to care about books and other kinds of reading materials. Let's hope you will use the ideas to inspire them to write, draw, paint, and sculpt—in a word, create. Literacy is such an important part of our lives. It has kept my family close, and it can do the same for yours, especially if you follow the advice in this valuable book.

Norman Bridwell, creator of Clifford the Big Red Dog®

Introduction

We've all seen the PSAs. Movie stars, athletes, and politicians encouraging us to read to our children. Read to our children. Read to our children. We get it: We should read to our children! Unfortunately, though, 15-second public service announcements too often leave us asking, "*What* am I supposed to read?" "*How* am I supposed to read?" "*When* am I supposed to read?" "Are there activities in addition to reading that will boost my child's literacy?" And, most important, "Why does this matter so much?" This book will answer all those questions, and, we hope, make you recognize what you are already doing to support your child in making literacy an important part of his life.

What This Book Won't Do

Although this book is crammed with useful ideas and information about developing literacy, it will not show you how to teach your child to read in 100 easy lessons before she is 3. It will not give you evidence to claim that your child is the best and brightest at the day care center. It will not allow you to skip getting that teaching certificate and become your school district's literacy coach. In a nutshell, the book is not a magic bullet but a useful tool to help you understand what is going on as your child is growing and how to support that growth.

Shannon Poynter

What This Book Will Do

This book is designed to help you, the interested parent, learn more about the seemingly magical process of literacy development. It will provide you with the guidelines you need to assist your young child in developing the skills and understandings that will allow him to make literacy a lifelong, enjoyable endeavor.

You will learn to develop a literacy-enriched environment for your child by thinking about the materials you provide and the access your child has to those materials. You will think about the role that literacy plays in your own life and discover ways to show how important it is to your child. Through this book, you will learn the critical aspects of literacy that can be developed birth to 5 and what you can do to address them.

We will help you consider many ways that literacy already touches your life and your child's—ways that you might not even be aware of. The bottom line: We will teach you to enhance what you are already doing and suggest new things to do to maximize the impact on your child's growing literacy.

Shannon Poynter

How to Use This Book

This book can be read in whole or in parts. You might sit down and read it cover to cover. We're guessing, though, that if you have young children, you won't have time to do that! So feel free to read it in chapters or chunks, reflect on what you read, and revisit it. Each chapter not only addresses how to promote literacy in a different part of your home (kitchen, living room, bedroom, and so forth), but also addresses different aspects of promoting literacy, such as building vocabulary, helping children understand how books work, and making connections between letters and the sounds they represent. The book is filled with tips, checklists, and quick ideas to help you promote literacy in whatever ways make sense for you, your child, and your busy life together. However you use the book, your child's life will be richer for it.

What Are Those Symbols?

Throughout this book, we use the convention of showing the sounds in words by using letters bracketed by slashes—for example, when we mean the *sssss* sound we'll represent it like this: /s/. If we mean the letter itself, we'll use s. So we could say, for example, that the letter *c* sometimes stands for the /k/ sound and sometimes stands for the /s/ sound.

Even for Infants?

It may be clear why we address preschoolers and toddlers—but infants? As a matter of fact, we have evidence that infants can engage in literacy activity. Nell's daughter, for example, turned the pages of Melanie Walsh's board book *Do Monkeys Tweet?* at 3 months, and laughed at parts of Eric Carle's *The Very Busy Spider* at 6 months—and Nell has the video to prove it! Indeed, by the end of infancy, many children growing up in literacy-rich homes can pretend to read books, make letter-like marks (in finger paint, perhaps), and, most important, show a strong interest in reading and writing materials. Therefore, throughout the book, we discuss developmentally appropriate literacy-rich environments and activities for infants.

Marcel Charpentier

CHAPTER I

Literacy and the Young Child

Ellen Daugherty Durr

When You Say "Literacy," What Exactly Do You Mean?

Long ago, being literate meant being able to sign your name! Over time, the definition of literacy grew to mean the ability to read enough to get by in life and work, to write a little, and that was about it. As more time has passed, and society's demand for literacy has increased, that definition has changed radically. Literacy has come to mean reading, writing, listening, speaking, gaining meaning from pictures by viewing, and communicating ideas by visually representing them.[1] The current concept of literacy encompasses much more than knowing the alphabet or being able to sound out words; in fact, there are many children who can do those things but can't understand what they are reading, communicate effectively through writing, or use language to meet their needs or accomplish their goals. Later in this

Ryan J Verhey-Henke

What Is Emergent Literacy?

Emergent literacy refers to the point in children's development before they become conventionally literate—that is, before they can read on their own or write text that others can read.[2] The concept assumes literacy learning begins at birth and develops or emerges gradually over time. There is no magic moment when children suddenly "are readers and writers." They are always *becoming* readers and writers. Unlike "reading readiness," this view maintains that children are born ready to learn about literacy and continue to grow in their literacy understandings throughout life. Understanding emergent literacy is important for parents because it implies that the extent to which you support your child's literacy development in the early years of life is critical and consequential to success in later life.

chapter, we share specific literacy goals for children according to age, but fundamentally, we're concerned with developing skills—in reading, writing, listening, speaking, viewing, and visually representing—from the first moments babies can hear and see us. (See the section entitled Why Start So Early With Literacy? on page 15.) Regardless of your child's age, if he is growing in his ability to read, write, listen, speak, view, and visually represent, he is becoming literate, or developing *emergent literacy*. (See What Is Emergent Literacy? to the left.) The purpose of this book is to help you foster emergent literacy.

Literacy Development Begins at Birth

Educators used to believe there was a particular age when children were "ready to read." One study, published in 1931, even determined this magic age to be 6.5 years.[3] But more recent thinking suggests that literacy "emerges" from birth, given exposure to a literacy-rich environment. Long before children can read and write in the conventional sense, they are learning about literacy.[4] Specifically, they are learning why, what, and how people read.

Why People Read

Children first learn about literacy and its functions from the people around them. As your child's parent, you show her daily the many reasons for interacting with text. For example, when you bring in the mail, you might say, "I wonder what came today."

Reading Makes You Feel Good is a children's book about many of the different reasons we read.

You might find a letter from Grandma, a circular from the supermarket, a couple of bills, and a clothing catalog. Let your child see you read the letter, find out what's going on with Grandma, and maybe laugh at a funny story she tells. Let her see you read the circular, cut the coupons from it, and perhaps make a list of items to purchase. Let her see you pay the bills by writing a check, and let her look at the catalog herself. A single mail delivery provides many opportunities to show different reasons for reading and writing.

What People Read

Look around and notice all the different kinds of reading materials available to us—books, magazines, newspapers, Web sites, labels, signs, and so many others. Don't be surprised if your child is already aware of these materials. One of our favorite illustrations of how much young children can learn about different types of texts is from a 3-year-old child who scribble-wrote two texts—one with short scribbles in a narrow column down one side of the page, another with long scribbles that extend across the page. She identified the former as a shopping list and the latter as a story! Already she knew something about these two different kinds of text. (See samples to the right.)

A 3-year-old's "shopping list" and "story."
(From J. C. Harste, V. A. Woodward, and C. L. Burke's *Language Stories & Literacy Lessons*)

How People Read

Children begin to learn about how we read as early as infancy. Specifically, they develop concepts of print, basic understandings of how print "works," alphabet knowledge, comprehension skills, and other literacy knowledge and abilities. For example, they learn that we:

* Read (English) from left to right and top to bottom
* Identify words by looking at their letters, which in turn represent sounds in speech

* Use different parts of the text—such as words, illustrations, graphics, and the context of reading—to help us make meaning

(For further discussion of children's growing knowledge about how to read, see Chapter 3.)

So often, people think about a young child as a prereader or nonreader and don't pay much attention to what he already knows about reading. The same goes for writing. But researchers who have studied children's early attempts at composition have made some fascinating discoveries about children's knowledge.[5] Consider the example below. This child has already learned so much about literacy. She has learned that

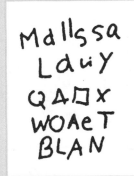   

A child's birthday list, map, letter, and story page. (From J. C. Harste, V. A. Woodward, and C. L. Burke's *Language Stories & Literacy Lessons*)

we use print to keep track of things (birthday list), inform (map), communicate (letter), and entertain (story page). She has learned that we use letters in written language, what the relationship is between sounds and letters (for example, the letter *m* stands for the sound /m/), and even the conventional spellings for some words (for example, *love* and her own name). She knows that we use spaces to separate words, that we write and read from left to right and top to bottom on a page. She knows that a list is usually a single column of words or phrases on a common topic, and that a letter often begins with a salutation ("Dear Mom"), ends with a closing statement ("Love Steph"), and contains a personal message. She even knows that we often write letters on decorative stationery! She knows that a map tells us how to get to or find places and that, on a map, words are intermingled with graphics. In contrast, on her story page, she separates the words and the graphics, but maintains a thematic relationship, as story writers often do. And this analysis doesn't even cover all this child knows about literacy! Take a look at your own child's writing and don't be surprised if there's a lot more to it than you initially believed.

Why Start So Early With Literacy?

Why is it so important to provide literacy-rich environments and activities for young children? Why should we put them on the road to reading and writing as early as infancy? Here are five reasons, although there are undoubtedly many more.

Literacy Can Enrich Your Child's Daily Life

Just as print plays an integral role in your life, it can play an integral role in your child's life as well. For example, name labels can identify your child's clothing, room, and artwork. Labels and pictures can indicate where materials and toys are stored. A list of your child's favorite foods can be used to plan meals together. Reading aloud daily can be engaging for children—just as engaging as dressing up, building with blocks, or playing on a jungle gym. Literacy is so embedded in the homes featured in this book that it is impossible to imagine what life would be like without it.

Literacy Can Be a Source of Great Joy for Your Child

For generations children have enjoyed wonderful books such as *The Snowy Day* by Ezra Jack Keats, *The Runaway Bunny* by Margaret Wise Brown, first-word books, and many others. We have never met a preschooler who did not respond with glee to the playful book *Tumble Bumble* by Felicia Bond. We have never met an infant who was not captivated by Margaret Miller's *Baby Faces*. Many adults can still tell you their favorite children's book. In fact, certain children's authors, such as Dr. Seuss and Maurice Sendak, conjure up so much nostalgia, they have become a permanent part of adult popular culture. All children have a right to the joy that books and beloved authors can bring.

Literacy Provides a Way for Your Child to Learn About the World

Books and other print materials can help children explore and better understand the people, places, and things that they encounter in everyday life. Print can also help children learn about the bigger world beyond their immediate one. Children on a farm in Iowa can learn about people who live near the ocean in California. Children who live in the United States can learn about the history and culture of people in China. Children everywhere can learn about dinosaurs, the moon, and life underground. Literacy, like nothing else, puts the whole world in children's hands.

Literacy Knowledge Is an Excellent Predictor of Your Child's Later School Achievement

Children who know alphabet letters and the sounds they represent, who can separate and blend sounds and groups of sounds that make up words, who have rich vocabulary and concept knowledge, and who understand how print works are far more likely to be good readers in kindergarten and in the grades that follow.[6] And this connection is not just coincidental but causal. Providing stronger language and literacy education for children in the early years has been shown to lead to better outcomes for them later on.[7]

Literacy Builds Knowledge About the Way Language Works

Books and other print materials are important tools for building children's vocabulary. Our language contains many words and complex structures that children may not learn unless they are exposed to books and other print materials. Everyday oral language often does not include all of the words and language structures we find in written text. Consider the following passages from two children's books:

Tiptoeing with solemn face,

with some flowers and a vase,

in they walked and then said, "Ahhh,"

when they saw the toys and candy

and the dollhouse from Papa.

From *Madeline* by Ludwig Bemelmans

Something big stirred underneath her. Daisy shivered.

She scrambled up onto the riverbank. Then something

screeched in the sky above!

From *Come Along, Daisy!* by Jane Simmons

These books, each appropriate even for toddlers, have wonderfully rich vocabulary and sentence constructions. Hearing books like these helps children develop powerful and sophisticated language that will be important to them in their own writing in later schooling, in their careers, and in other communications.[8]

The arguments for weaving literacy into young children's environments and activities are multiple and strong. However, some educators and parents worry that introducing literacy is not developmentally appropriate for young children. As you might guess, we disagree.

What Should You Expect to See as Your Child Grows From Infant to Kindergartener?

If we agree that literacy begins developing right from birth, a next logical question is: What should we expect from children at different ages? What should children know and be able to do in literacy when they leave infancy and enter toddlerhood? Leave toddlerhood and enter preschool? How about by the end of preschool? Having the answers may help you engage your child in developmentally appropriate activities and build on her emergent literacy (as will reading this book, we hope).

Developing Literacy *Is* Part of Developing the Whole Child

Early childhood educators often talk of developing "the whole child," meaning not just one or two aspects of the child but all areas: cognitive, physical, socio-emotional, linguistic, and creative. Until recently though, literacy has not been a big part of planning for young children. In fact, the position statement on developmentally appropriate practice from National Association for the Development of Young Children (NAEYC) has changed significantly over the last decade—from a passing reference to providing young children with literacy experiences[9] to a clear recommendation that emphasizes the importance of including carefully planned literacy experiences in programs for young children.[10]

As parents, we are committed to ensuring that our children reach a whole host of developmental milestones—from learning to eat their vegetables to independently dressing themselves to developing values we care about. We're also committed to doing everything we can to help our children reach those milestones. Should literacy be part of that mix? Even in the preschool years? Experts believe it should. Literacy is important to many aspects of daily life. Although we do not want to see a focus on literacy detract from developing children in other areas, literacy has to be one of our primary concerns as parents.

Goals for Birth to 3-Years-Old, 3- to 4-Years-Old, and Kindergarten

Like developmental milestones in any area, literacy milestones will vary by individual child and depend on the experiences he has had. A child who has been provided with literacy-rich activities and environments from birth is likely to reach milestones more quickly and even exceed them. What follows are goals established by organizations that are committed to promoting effective and appropriate research-based literacy practices. Of course, every child is different, so don't panic if your child is below or above these goals. Use these goals as guidelines to think about how you can enrich or challenge your child's literacy development. Some of the language in these goals may be unfamiliar but it will become clearer later in the book.

Birth to Three-Year-Old Accomplishments[11]

* Recognizes specific books by cover.
* Pretends to read books.
* Understands that books are handled in particular ways.
* Enters into a book-sharing routine with primary caregivers.
* Vocalization play in crib gives way to enjoyment of rhyming language, nonsense wordplay, etc.

- Labels objects in books.
- Comments on characters in books.
- Looks at picture in book and realizes it is a symbol for a real object.
- Listens to stories.
- Requests/commands adult to read or write.
- May begin attending to specific print, such as letters in names.
- Uses increasingly purposeful scribbling.
- Occasionally seems to distinguish between drawing and writing.
- Produces some letter-like forms and scribbles with some features of English writing.

Three- to Four-Year-Old Accomplishments[12]

Book Appreciation and Knowledge

- Shows interest in shared reading experiences and looking at books independently.
- Recognizes how books are read, such as front-to-back and one page at a time, and recognizes basic characteristics, such as title, author, and illustrator.

Michael Kozura

- Asks and answers questions and makes comments about print materials.

Should My Child Be Reading Before Kindergarten?

In a word, *no*. Although some children will be reading—able to decode words and understand their collective meaning—most will not. And this is *fine*. Although expectations for kindergarteners have been ramped up significantly from when we were young, children are still not expected to read *before* kindergarten. In most places, they are expected to be able to read some simple texts by the end of kindergarten. Your child's kindergarten teacher should be able to tell you about the expectations in your area.

That said, preschoolers *can* acquire knowledge and skills that put them on the road to reading. The goals on pages 17–28 tell you what to expect. Your community may have a set of guidelines of its own, which you might obtain by contacting the principal of your local elementary school or your school district's central office. In any case, we believe that the majority of children will be prepared for kindergarten if you carry out over time the kinds of activities suggested in this book.

Should I Teach My Child to Read Before Kindergarten?

This depends on what you mean by "teach." If you mean the kinds of activities recommended throughout this book, then certainly, yes. You can do many things to teach your child to read—from frequently reading aloud to him to spelling words when he asks you to. But if you mean giving your child reading "lessons," drilling with flashcards, assigning phonics worksheets, having him work through a commercial program ("Teach your child to read in 10 easy steps . . ."), then our answer is no. Why?

* **You are your child's parent, first and foremost.** There are a number of pitfalls that arise when you try to mix the role of parent with the role of teacher. Of course, there are parents who choose to homeschool and, therefore, take on both roles, but these parents usually spend considerable time figuring out how to manage the two roles, how to avoid the pitfalls, and so on. It does not make a lot of sense to take all this on when the child needn't be reading yet anyway!

* **Most likely, you are not qualified.** Although you undoubtedly have a lot to offer your child, you probably have not received formal training in literacy education. In contrast, your child's kindergarten and first-grade teachers probably have, and probably also have materials developed to teach reading, so leave the formal reading instruction to them.

* **Childhood is a journey, not a race.** Although it may impress friends and neighbors, reading early offers no tremendous benefit to a child. As we show throughout this book, your child can derive great pleasure from literacy before she can read conventionally, and there are important areas of literacy—such as vocabulary and comprehension—that can develop without her being able to read in the conventional sense. In the long run, it probably doesn't matter a whole lot whether your child has learned to read before or after beginning formal schooling.

* **Negative attitudes can result.** Teaching your child to read conventionally before he is ready may, however unintentionally, place too much pressure on him. The very last thing we want is to send children to school with negative associations with literacy—we don't want them feeling unsuccessful, overwhelmed, or pressured because of the "teaching" they've received, in which they've been expected to learn to read or write conventionally too early.

* **Bad habits can result.** When trying to accomplish something that is too difficult for us, we sometimes develop bad habits. For example, if you are skiing down a slope that is much too steep for you, you may find yourself using poor form to get to the mountain base without falling. If you are learning a new language too quickly, you may develop bad pronunciation that will be difficult to undo later on.

Similarly, if a child is taught to read formally too soon, she may develop bad habits. For example, she may try to recognize words by their shape, guess at words without considering their letters and/or context, or form letters in inefficient ways. Of course, children may adopt some or all of these strategies in the normal course of development, but these tendencies should not be bolstered by presenting tasks that are too difficult or out of sync with your child's development.

Of course, if your child asks questions about how to read or write one word or many, or what something means, you should gladly answer those questions. And, naturally, you should provide the rich literacy environments and experiences described in this book. But save the formal "lessons" for later!

* Demonstrates interest in different kinds of literature, such as fiction and non-fiction books and poetry, on a range of topics.

* Retells stories or information from books through conversation, artistic works, creative movement, or drama.

Phonological Awareness

* Identifies and discriminates between words in language.

* Identifies and discriminates between separate syllables in words.

* Identifies and discriminates between sounds and phonemes in language, such as attention to beginning and ending sounds of words and recognition that different words begin or end with the same sound.

Alphabet Knowledge

* Recognizes that the letters of the alphabet are a special category of visual graphics that can be individually named.

* Recognizes that letters of the alphabet have distinct sounds associated with them.

* Attends to the beginning letters and sounds in familiar words.

* Identifies letters and associates correct sounds with letters.

Print Concepts and Conventions

* Recognizes print in everyday life, such as numbers, letters, one's name, words, and familiar logos and signs.

* Understands that print conveys meaning.

* Understands conventions, such as print moves from left to right and top to bottom of a page.

* Recognizes words as a unit of print and understands that letters are grouped to form words.

* Recognizes the association between spoken or signed and written words.

Early Writing

* Experiments with writing tools and materials.

* Recognizes that writing is a way of communicating for a variety of purposes, such as giving information, sharing stories, or giving an opinion.

* Uses scribbles, shapes, pictures, and letters to represent objects, stories, experiences, or ideas.

* Copies, traces, or independently writes letters or words.

Receptive Language

* Attends to language during conversations, songs, stories, or other learning experiences.

* Comprehends increasingly complex and varied vocabulary.

* Comprehends different forms of language, such as questions or exclamations.

* Comprehends different grammatical structures or rules for using language.

Expressive Language

* Engages in communication and conversation with others.

* Uses language to express ideas and needs.

* Uses increasingly complex and varied vocabulary.

* Uses different forms of language.

* Uses different grammatical structures for a variety of purposes.

* Engages in storytelling.

* Engages in conversations with peers and adults.

Kindergarten Accomplishments[13]

These are expectations for the end of kindergarten. Use them as guidelines as you think about literacy development.

Reading Literature

Key Ideas and Details

* With prompting and support, asks and answers questions about key details in a text.

* With prompting and support, retells familiar stories, including key details.

* With prompting and support, identifies characters, settings, and major events in a story.

Craft and Structure

* Asks and answers questions about unknown words in a text.
* Recognizes common types of texts (e.g., storybooks, poems).
* With prompting and support, names the author and illustrator of a story and defines the role of each in telling the story.

Integration of Knowledge and Ideas

* With prompting and support, describes the relationship between illustrations and the story in which they appear (e.g., what moment in a story an illustration depicts).
* With prompting and support, compares and contrasts the adventures and experiences of characters in familiar stories.

Range of Reading and Level of Text Complexity

* Actively engages in group reading activities with purpose and understanding.

Reading Informational Text
Key Ideas and Details

* With prompting and support, asks and answers questions about key details in a text.
* With prompting and support, identifies the main topic and retells key details of a text.
* With prompting and support, describes the connection between two individuals, events, ideas, or pieces of information in a text.

Craft and Structure

* With prompting and support, asks and answers questions about unknown words in a text.
* Identifies the front cover, back cover, and title page of a book.
* Names the author and illustrator of a text and defines the role of each in presenting the ideas or information in a text.

Integration of Knowledge and Ideas

* With prompting and support, describes the relationship between illustrations and the text in which they appear (e.g., what person, place, thing, or idea in the text an illustration depicts).

* With prompting and support, identifies the reasons an author gives to support points in a text.

* With prompting and support, identifies basic similarities in and differences between two texts on the same topic (e.g., in illustrations, descriptions, or procedures).

Range of Reading and Level of Text Complexity

* Actively engages in group reading activities with purpose and understanding.

Foundational Skills

Print Concepts

* Demonstrates understanding of the organization and basic features of print.

  ◇ Follows words from left to right, top to bottom, and page by page.

  ◇ Recognizes that spoken words are represented in written language by specific sequences of letters.

  ◇ Understands that words are separated by spaces in print.

  ◇ Recognizes and names all upper- and lowercase letters of the alphabet.

Phonological Awareness

* Demonstrates understanding of spoken words, syllables, and sounds (phonemes).

  ◇ Recognizes and produces rhyming words.

  ◇ Counts, pronounces, blends, and segments the syllables in spoken words.

  ◇ Blends and segments onsets and rimes (initial sounds and those that follow) of single-syllable spoken words.

- ◇ Isolates and pronounces the initial, medial vowel, and final sounds (phonemes) in three-phoneme (consonant-vowel-consonant, or CVC) words. (This does not include CVCs ending with /l/, /r/, or /x/.)
- ◇ Adds or substitutes individual sounds (phonemes) in simple, one-syllable words to make new words.

Phonics and Word Recognition

- ✳ Knows and applies grade-level phonics and word analysis skills in decoding words.
  - ◇ Demonstrates basic knowledge of one-to-one letter-sound correspondences by producing the primary, or many of the most frequent, sounds for each consonant.
  - ◇ Associates the long and short sounds with common spellings (graphemes) for the five major vowels.
  - ◇ Reads common high-frequency words by sight (e.g., *the, of, to, you, she, my, is, are, do, does*).
  - ◇ Distinguishes between similarly spelled words by identifying the sounds of the letters that differ.

Fluency

  - ◇ Reads emergent-reader texts (materials written for the earliest readers) with purpose and understanding.

Writing

Text Types and Purposes

- ✳ Uses a combination of drawing, dictating, and writing to compose opinion pieces in which she tells a reader the topic or the name of the book she is writing about and states an opinion or preference about the topic or book (e.g., *My favorite book is…*).
- ✳ Uses a combination of drawing, dictating, and writing to compose informative/explanatory texts in which he names what he is writing about and supplies some information about the topic.

* Uses a combination of drawing, dictating, and writing to narrate a single event or several loosely linked events, tell about the events in the order in which they occurred, and provide a reaction to what happened.

Production and Distribution of Writing

* With guidance and support from adults, responds to questions and suggestions from peers and adds details to strengthen writing as needed.
* With guidance and support from adults, explores a variety of digital tools to produce and publish writing, including in collaboration with peers.

Research to Build and Present Knowledge

* Participates in shared research and writing projects (e.g., explores a number of books by a favorite author and expresses opinions about them).
* With guidance and support from adults, recalls information from experiences or gathers information from provided sources to answer a question.

Speaking and Listening

Comprehension and Collaboration

* Participates in collaborative conversations with diverse partners about *kindergarten topics and texts* with peers and adults in small and larger groups.
  * Follows agreed-upon rules for discussions (e.g., listening to others and taking turns speaking about the topics and texts under discussion).
  * Continues a conversation through multiple exchanges.
* Confirms understanding of a text read aloud or information presented orally or through other media by asking and answering questions about key details and requesting clarification if something is not understood.
* Asks and answers questions in order to seek help, get information, or clarify something that is not understood.

Presentation of Knowledge and Ideas

* Describes familiar people, places, things, and events and, with prompting and support, provides additional detail.

* Adds drawings or other visual displays to descriptions as desired to provide additional detail.

* Speaks audibly and expresses thoughts, feelings, and ideas clearly.

Language

Conventions of Standard English

* Demonstrates command of the conventions of standard English grammar and usage when writing or speaking.

  ◇ Prints many upper- and lowercase letters.

  ◇ Uses frequently occurring nouns and verbs.

  ◇ Forms regular plural nouns orally by adding /s/ or /es/ (e.g., *dog, dogs; wish, wishes*).

  ◇ Understands and uses question words (interrogatives) (e.g., *who, what, where, when, why, how*).

  ◇ Uses the most frequently occurring prepositions (e.g., *to, from, in, out, on, off, for, of, by, with*).

  ◇ Produces and expands complete sentences in shared language activities.

* Demonstrates command of the conventions of standard English capitalization, punctuation, and spelling when writing.

  ◇ Capitalizes the first word in a sentence and the pronoun *I*.

  ◇ Recognizes and names end punctuation.

  ◇ Writes a letter or letters for most consonant and short-vowel sounds (phonemes).

  ◇ Spells simple words phonetically, drawing on knowledge of sound–letter relationships.

Vocabulary Acquisition and Use

* Determines or clarifies the meaning of unknown and multiple-meaning words and phrases *based on kindergarten reading and content.*

- ◇ Identifies new meanings for familiar words and applies them accurately (e.g., knowing *duck* is a bird and learning the verb *to duck*).

- ◇ Uses the most frequently occurring inflections and affixes (e.g., *-ed, -s, re-, un-, pre-, -ful, -less*) as clues to the meaning of an unknown word.

∗ With guidance and support from adults, explores word relationships and nuances in word meanings.

- ◇ Sorts common objects into categories (e.g., shapes, foods) to gain a sense of the concepts the categories represent.

- ◇ Demonstrates understanding of frequently occurring verbs and adjectives by relating them to their opposites (antonyms).

- ◇ Identifies real-life connections between words and their use (e.g., notes places at school that are *colorful*).

- ◇ Distinguishes shades of meaning among verbs describing the same general action (e.g., *walk, march, strut, prance*) by acting out the meanings.

∗ Uses words and phrases acquired through conversations, reading and being read to, and responding to texts.

Looking at long lists of expectations like these can be overwhelming. It can be frustrating, too, if you feel they over- or underestimate what children should know and be able to do, or when they seem to contradict other references. At the same time, these lists do provide a starting point for thinking through your own expectations. As you read this book, we hope you will identify your expectations and compare them to this list. Although our expectations are high, they are also attainable with well-planned, appropriate, and responsive literacy activities.

Why Do Families Matter?

You may be wondering why this book is addressed to parents and not teachers. We agree that teachers, including childcare providers, play an important role in developing young children's emergent literacy, and we have written a book for them: *Literacy and the Youngest Learner: Best Practices for Educators of Children From Birth to 5.*[14] But we believe that you, too, play a critical role. As your child's primary caregiver, you are uniquely positioned to maximize her growing literacy. You know your child better than anyone . . . better than her doctor, teacher, or child care provider. You recognize her signs of stress, excitement, and delight. You know her passions, curiosities, and motivations. You are familiar with the places she goes in a day. You are the one she goes to with interesting questions, stories of a great day at school, or tears after a conflict with a friend.

You are an expert on your child. As such, you have a ton of inside information that can help you think about what your child needs to develop skills, learn about the world, and fall in love with literacy. Most important, your loving connection to your child makes what matters to *you* matter to your child. Your valuing literacy "sells" it to your little one.

As your child's primary caregiver, you also have a great opportunity to demonstrate multiple purposes for literacy. Children need to understand that reading and writing are done for lots of reasons. At home, you can show your child real reasons that we read: to learn about something from the newspaper, to answer a question by "Googling" it, to enjoy a story, to decide which programs to watch on TV, to find a new store on your phone's map, to follow a recipe for dinner, to figure out how to put together a piece of furniture, to decide which coupons to cut, or to pay a bill, for example. You can also show many reasons we write: to e-mail a party invitation to a friend, to make a grocery list, to notify a teacher of a food allergy, to label a photograph you text to Grandpa, to write a check, to write a thank-you note to Grandma. Some teachers work hard to design authentic activities similar to these; they may come more naturally at home. Just as elementary teachers do, you can model; you can teach explicitly; you can guide your child's attempts at understanding new words and ideas; and you can provide opportunities for independent practice.

YOUR ROLE

You may have heard that dining as a family is closely correlated with children's academic success.[15] Family members who dine together talk to one another, ask questions, listen, ask for and provide more information, model language use, and make connections between ideas and experiences. But it's not eating together per se that leads to academic success. Rather, it's what happens at the table while eating: rich communication that, at its best, gets beyond the here and now. And that communication can happen anywhere. What's most important is that it happens. Research also shows that children from families that use rich language at dinner have better vocabularies and can draw on those vocabularies throughout life, including while learning to read.[16] Consider this conversation from Susan's house:

DAD: How was school today, Violet?

VIOLET (age 5): Fine.

DAD: What did you play?

VIOLET: I painted.

DAD: Did you paint with anyone?

VIOLET: Yeah, Jackson painted with me.

DAD: Were you working on the same painting?

VIOLET: No, I was on one side, and he was on the other.

DAD: On the other side of the easel?

VIOLET: Yeah, the easel.

Although this is not the most scintillating conversation, there is power in its simplicity. Violet is learning that more detail can help a listener better understand what she is talking about. She also learned that the thing you clip paper to for painting is called an easel. She had the chance to engage in conversational turn-taking, listening for questions and then answering after her dad was finished. All of this was said in less than a minute. Her dad didn't have any lesson plan in mind, but rather a sincere desire to understand Violet's day and connect with her during dinner.

Dinner-table conversations are just one small way to build our children's literacy. This book shows you other ways. It will help you find little pockets of time through-out your day to enrich literacy through conversation and other activities.

Concluding Thoughts

We hope this chapter has helped convince you, or affirmed your belief, that literacy development begins at birth, and that important literacy knowledge and skills emerge—depending on the quality of environments and activities—from the beginning of your child's life. We also hope that you believe, as we do, that it is important to focus on literacy from birth to kindergarten (and beyond) not just because it prepares children for later life, but because of the enjoyment and stimulation that literacy offers them now. In the next chapter, we discuss specific areas of early literacy learning and our overall vision for how the home environment can help children accomplish this learning. There are so many ways to build literacy in young children. Let's explore them!

The Research Says...

You already know how important you are to your child. In recent years, many studies have reinforced the idea that a family's involvement in their child's learning can make a big difference for the child.[17] Did you know the following?

* Children whose parents have higher expectations for them tend to achieve more in school.[18]
* Similarly, children whose parents expect more of them expect more of themselves and tend to do better in school.[19]
* Children whose parents read with them regularly value reading themselves and tend to be better readers.[20]
* Children who have better vocabularies find learning to read to be easier. The development of a child's vocabulary is closely linked to the vocabulary of her parents and how they use that vocabulary.[21]
* Families are uniquely positioned to help their children learn about their world. Children who have more prior knowledge about given topics connect better to texts about those topics and are more motivated to learn.[22]

CHAPTER 2

Literacy Throughout the Day

*H*ow many different ways have you included literacy in your day since you woke up this morning? Did you read the news on your tablet? Prepare muffins from a mix? Check your e-mail? Sign homework for your older child? Watch the news for the weather forecast? Follow road signs while driving? So much of what we do is driven by text that we often don't realize just how much we are, in fact, reading and writing on a daily basis. What we propose is weaving literacy into your children's lives in the same way. Actually, in all likelihood, you're already doing that. What we are *really* proposing, then, is that you call attention to the text in your child's world and help him or her interact with it further.

Ellen Daugherty Durr

Literacy, Literacy, Everywhere!

Just as you have text coming at you all day long, so do children. The difference is they may not realize that text has meaning—whether that text is a one-word traffic sign or a Russian novel—or that that meaning is important to them. Our environments are full of objects, and over time we learn that some objects are more worthy of our attention than others. For example, the signs that indicate whether a bathroom is for males or females are important to pay attention to; the screws that hold the bathroom door on its frame are usually not. At first, your child may pay no more (or perhaps even less) attention to the signs on the bathroom doors than she does to the screws that hold on those doors. But over time, especially if you point them out and help your child understand their meaning and importance, she will attend carefully to those signs. The more opportunity children have to learn about the meaning and importance of the print around them, the more attentive to, and comfortable with, this print they'll become.

It's important to note that reading isn't "natural." Children don't develop the ability to read and write like they develop a full set of teeth. Reading and writing must be taught, like good manners, game rules, and the names of the planets. As parents, you spend a great deal of time helping your child make her way in the world by teaching her all kinds of things she needs to know: Hold hands when you cross the street; say "please" when you want something; don't talk to strangers; and so forth. Another enormous contribution you can make to her development is to teach her about literacy. Help her become comfortable and able to move freely through our text-saturated culture.

Because we do live in such a text-rich culture, we have many opportunities to share that print with our children. Everywhere we turn, morning, noon, and night, there is print—print that we can read with our children, create with our children, talk about with our children. It is for this reason that we suggest that you use a literacy-throughout-the-day approach to help your child become the best reader, writer, and communicator he can be.

The Literacy-Throughout-the-Day Approach: Why Does It Matter?

Quite simply, this approach links literacy to most everything you do with your child all day, in a natural, enjoyable way. Why does this matter for young children?

Young Children Learn Best Through Repeated Exposure to Materials and Experiences

By offering literacy opportunities throughout the day, your child can visit the same books or activities again and again, thereby becoming comfortable with text and aware of some of its characteristics. For example, if you read *Goldilocks and the Three Bears* by James Marshall at bedtime and then have flannel board pieces or puppets of the main characters available the next day, you may find your child moving the pieces around mimicking your telling of the story. In her retelling, she may include voices for different characters; a problem and resolution; and conventional story language such as "Once upon a time" and "They lived happily ever after." All of these behaviors show a familiarity with stories.

Young Children May Learn About All Kinds of Reading Materials

By incorporating literacy into experiences beyond bedtime stories, you may be more inclined to include types of text or genres other than fiction. For example, you might include newspaper flyers in a pretend grocery store so that your child can see coupons, sales information, and item labels. You might supply

Raymond Coutu

informational texts about rocks if your child starts a rock collection. You might put how-to books on block construction in the block basket so that he can try copying structures. Toddlers might enjoy seeing their favorite songs written out on big paper, with picture cues for gestures. All of these text-based activities expose children to more than stories. Experiences with multiple genres have proven to be beneficial to primary-grade children, particularly in their ability to produce their own informational text.[23] Preschool children, too, seem to learn about the genres to which they're exposed.[24] Early experience with a variety of texts is beneficial to children.

Young Children Gain Literacy Regardless of the Activity They Choose

You may have a child who never leaves a particular activity. In our classroom, we had one boy who refused to leave his block building . . . ever. Luring him to the book corner would have taken a miracle. But because we had reading and writing materials throughout our classroom, he could stay in the block area and still be exposed to important literacy-building opportunities. Stocking the area with books on architecture and construction, labeling the block shelves with shape names ("square," "small rectangle," "large rectangle," "triangle," "wedge," etc.), and providing a clipboard and graph paper for documenting the buildings children created all reinforced what this child was doing but also helped him build a solid foundation of literacy. You can certainly employ the same strategy at home. If your "train guy" can't let go of his Thomas the Tank Engine toys, how might you incorporate text into his play? Might you find books on trains? Map his track? Label the cars with their "contents"? Provide paper for him to make his own signs for destinations? What else might you do?

If every room and activity similarly incorporates literacy, your child will have a chance to interact with it on his own terms and level of interest.

Young Children Spend More Time Building Skills

As you will learn in the upcoming chapters, most read-aloud experiences last only a few minutes (as they should). We think children need more exposure to literacy than to share a few short books at bedtime. Providing that exposure throughout the day ensures a rich literacy environment that supports children's literacy knowledge much better than a few three-minute read-alouds can. More, in this case, really is better.

Finally, weaving literacy into the whole day is just plain fun for everyone! Some of our fondest memories are of the times we truly communicated with our children—talking about a magazine, finding out the answer to a puzzled 3-year-old's question, or singing silly songs. We hope you'll find these experiences enjoyable as well.

What Are You Already Doing... and What Are You Not?

In Chapter 1, we defined literacy as reading, writing, listening, speaking, viewing, and visually representing. Given that collection of behaviors, we argue that it is more difficult *not* to engage in literacy-building experiences throughout the day than to engage in them. As adults, we are always talking, listening, reading, or writing. We gain meaning from viewing graphs and pictures regularly. Many adults don't seize opportunities to represent their ideas visually through drawing, but children certainly do. This literate life swirls around your child all day long.

Even though the child who drew this could write some letters, she chose to draw a picture to represent how she and her friends felt about her upcoming move out of state. According to the child, the floating signs in the background say "sad," represented as frowns.

The repeating frowns on the back of the picture, which morph into cursive-like scribbles, also say "sad," according to the child.

Throughout this book we offer activities that can be conducted in your home, in your vehicle, or out in the world—anywhere you and your child are together. First, though, you should find out what you already *are* doing to promote literacy for your child so that you can focus on the things you're *not* doing. The Home Literacy Behavior Checklist on the following two pages helps you do just that. It's not exhaustive, but it does cover some of the major areas you should be thinking about, and we provide help throughout the book, whether you feel you have a lot or a little more to do.

The Home Literacy Behavior Checklist

Take a mental inventory. . . . What are you already doing with your child to promote his literacy learning? The checklist below gives you some ideas about how to provide a literacy-enriched home.

After you complete the checklist, you may find that you feel great about all that you are already doing with your child. Even so, you may find some new ideas that you hadn't considered and aren't sure how to facilitate. If this is the case, fear not; throughout this book you will find support.

Creating a Literacy-Rich Home Environment

- ☐ Can my child see a great deal of print in our home, such as in magazines, books, newspapers, and letters?
- ☐ Do I provide a variety of types of texts, such as storybooks, rhyming books, informational books, concept books, and cookbooks?
- ☐ Is there a special area that is designed especially for reading books together?
- ☐ Do I have books or other print material in every room in our home?
- ☐ Do I use and encourage my child to use this print?
- ☐ Do I make different texts available often?

Promoting Oral Language

- ☐ Do I provide opportunities to talk with my child?
- ☐ Do I really listen to my child?
- ☐ Do I convey an interest in what my child wants to share?
- ☐ Does my child hear more than just directives from me? (e.g. "stop," "sit down")
- ☐ Do I use interesting new vocabulary with my child?
- ☐ Do I explain unfamiliar words to my child to build vocabulary?
- ☐ Do I provide language for what my child is thinking or doing?
- ☐ Do I tell and draw out stories for my child?
- ☐ Do I sing songs and share nursery rhymes with my child?
- ☐ Do we enjoy children's songs, poems, stories, nursery rhymes, and informational (factual) texts in print and electronically?

Raymond Coutu

continued on the next page

Engaging in Read-Alouds

☐ Do I read aloud to my child every day?

☐ Do I make sure that read-aloud time is comfortable and unrushed?

☐ Do I read with expression?

☐ Do I model that I am having fun reading aloud?

☐ When I read aloud, is it interactive, with many opportunities for my child to share observations and ask questions?

☐ Do I run my finger under the words as I read and draw my child's attention to print and how books "work"?

☐ Do I point out letters for my child to identify?

☐ Do I help my child understand what we read by making connections to my child's life, other books we have shared, or something we know about the world?

☐ Do I reread some of my child's favorites?

☐ Do I introduce my child to new books and other texts?

Promoting Writing

☐ Do I provide my child with materials for writing and drawing, such as a variety of papers, pencils, markers, crayons, keyboard and mouse, and touchscreen?

☐ Do I encourage my child to write and draw?

☐ Do I encourage my child to write his or her name on the paper and praise whatever that looks like?

☐ Do I ask my child to read to me what he or she has written?

☐ Do I model writing in front of my child, discussing what I'm doing (for example, answering e-mail, paying a bill, writing a letter)?

☐ Do I display my child's writing and other work?

Other Literacy Activities

☐ Do I have materials that allow my child to manipulate letters (for example, magnetic letters on the refrigerator, alphabet sponges in the tub, or rubber stamps and paper)?

☐ Do I provide audio books or book-based videos?

☐ Do I offer e-books on a computer or mobile device?

☐ Do I play games with my child that include some literacy?

☐ Does my child have access to puppets and other ways to act out stories?

☐ Do I use interactive literacy apps with my child in moderation?

☐ Do I encourage my child to incorporate print in his or her pretend play?

☐ Do I take my child on walks or other outings and talk about the print we see?

☐ When I cook, do I allow my child to help read the recipe and prepare the food?

☐ What else do I do to provide literacy opportunities for my child?

☐ What else do I do to encourage my child's love of literacy and learning?

What Skills Should Be Developed?

In addition to evaluating your child's literacy experiences, think about what he should be learning during these early years. The goals presented in Chapter 1 can be a guide for you, but within those goals are specific skills that you can help your child develop. We believe the following areas represent the range of what young children should be learning in literacy from birth to age 5:

* **Concepts of Print:** Concepts of print are some of the basic things that readers need to know about books and print. For example, children need to know that books have a front and a back. They need to be shown that, in English, we read from left to right. They also have to understand that the letters on a page make up words that have meaning, and that pictures can also help them understand what they're reading.

* **Phonological Awareness:** Phonological awareness is the ability to separate sounds and groups of sounds that make up words, such as the three sounds /sh/, /ee/, and /p/ in the word *sheep*. It does not directly involve letters; it has to do with hearing certain sounds within words and making those sounds. When children have strong phonological awareness, they can recognize when words rhyme, and they can come up with rhyming words. They can recognize when words start with the same sound and can think of words that start with the same sound. They can blend individual sounds together to form words and separate words into individual sounds. These skills eventually help children to use sounds to read and write words.

* **Oral Language:** Oral language has two parts. The first is the ability to talk, or communicate with language. The second is the ability to understand the language you hear. Vocabulary is a big part of oral language, which is why talking with children is so important—the more they hear words, the better able they are to understand and then use them. The strength of a child's oral language has a powerful influence on how well children learn to read and write.

SKILLS TO DEVELOP

* **Letter-Sound Knowledge:** Letter-sound knowledge refers to knowing the names and sounds of letters. For example, letter-sound knowledge means a child knows this shape—M— is called the letter *M* and stands for the *mmmmm* sound as at the beginning of *moon*. This can be tricky because there are 26 letters in the English alphabet that can be used alone or in combination to make about 44 sounds. Letter-sound knowledge eventually helps children to use letters to read the words that others have written and to represent the sounds they hear when writing words.

* **Comprehension:** Comprehension is the ability to make sense of the things that we see, read, and hear in the world around us. It is the purpose of reading. When we comprehend, we think about what we know already and how that relates to what we are seeing, reading, or hearing. We also think about what the author, illustrator, or speaker wants us to know.

* **Writing:** For young children, this means expressing meaning by drawing, scribbling, using pretend letters, using familiar letters and words, and using their best guesses as to how words might be spelled. These different types of writing allow children to communicate and to share their thinking with people who may not be present when they write.

* **Understandings of Genre:** This involves understanding that there are different kinds of text that have different features to serve different purposes. Genres young children might encounter include everything from street signs and menus to stories, information books, and poems.

* **Motivation to Interact With Print:** This refers to the desire to read, write, listen to, or otherwise interact with written language. Motivation is affected by a child's perception of the value of the activity (Is this worthwhile? Is this important?), the child's perception of himself (Am I good at this? Can I do this?), and other factors.

* **World Knowledge:** Literacy depends heavily on world knowledge. For example: "Sarah fell back on a cactus. 'Ouch!' she cried."

Here, it is knowledge of cacti that allows the reader or listener to infer that the spines of the cactus are what hurt the girl, leading her to say "Ouch!" Developing a greater store of world knowledge in young children helps them become better readers and writers later.

You'll find activities for promoting your child's abilities and under-standings of these areas throughout the book. Don't be surprised if, in some cases, you discover that you don't need to do anything different than what you're doing right now—or that you only need to make some slight refinements. For example, you may read to your baby every day. If so, keep doing that! You may want to help your toddler learn more from the read-aloud by pointing to the words as you read them. You could sweep your finger under the line of text as you read to help reinforce your child's growing understanding that we read from left to right—a fundamental concept of print. You could hand your baby the book upside down and praise her when she turns it right side up so you can read it. All of these simple moves help your child learn how books "work"— and build her literacy. (They're easy and do so much for your child.) This book will help you think carefully about how to turn what you are already doing into a purposeful plan for your child's literacy success.

Concluding Thoughts

From your earliest days together, you have done so much to help your child succeed in life. You monitor his diet and health, make sure he is clean and warm, supply him with educational materials to stimulate his mind. In addition to these basic things, you likely are already doing many things to promote her development in literacy as well. It's our hope that with this book in hand, you will start to become aware of all the different ways that literacy touches your life, all day, every day, and take advantage of those opportunities to give your child a solid, lifelong love of literacy and the skills needed to succeed not only in literacy but in life.

CHAPTER 3

Literacy Throughout the Home

Ellen Daugherty Durr

*H*ave you found yourself at the kitchen table reading the back of a cereal box for the third time? Or in a doctor's office waiting room reading a magazine that doesn't even interest you?

Or on the bus or train reading advertisements for products that you'd never buy in a million years? Why do you read these things? Because they are there! You can do a lot to increase your child's literacy simply by having print materials available throughout your home. In this chapter, we provide specific suggestions for enriching the literacy environment in your home. Specifically we discuss:

* Materials for reading

* Spaces for books and reading

* Materials for drawing and writing

Even if you are a die-hard bibliophile whose home is bursting at the seams with books, this chapter will provide you with fresh ideas and help you set the stage for the activities in the chapters that follow.

Buy the Book: Guidelines for Choosing Books Wisely

With so many books available for young children, it can be difficult to choose which ones to read. If you are borrowing from the library or otherwise spending little or no money on the books, the stakes are not quite as high, though even then, you don't want to select a bunch of "duds." If you are deciding on books to purchase, you want to be especially sure you don't pick too many disappointments. Here are some guidelines to consider when selecting books.

* **Look for authors and illustrators who are well known and/or well respected for their work.** Although there is no guarantee, books by authors and illustrators who are well known or books that have won honors or awards are more likely to be of high quality and satisfying for you and your child. Of course, what constitutes quality is somewhat subjective, but in general, honors and awards committees are looking for qualities similar to those you might care about: storybooks with rich language and a compelling plot; nonfiction books with fascinating as well as accurate information; and so on. Awards and honors to look for in picture books include the Boston Globe-Horn Book Award, the Caldecott Medal, the American Library Association's Notable Children's Books Award, the Coretta Scott King Award, the Parents' Choice Award, and the Reading Rainbow selection.

* **Be wary of mass-market books.** Mass-market books are available not only in bookstores—where they are often displayed on rotating racks rather than on the shelves—but in grocery stores, department store chains, and the like. There are some high-quality mass-market books, but many others are of poor quality. They are often based on toy, movie, and TV characters and written to capitalize on or perpetuate interest in those characters rather than to tell a good story or convey interesting information. The vocabulary, syntax, plot, illustrations, and other features are typically much less rich than you would find in award-winning and classic children's literature. Of course, if your child is really eager to have such a book, you may wish to consider buying it, but you should avoid putting too much time or money into these books at the expense of higher-quality selections.

* **Consider your child's interests and preferences.** One of your best guides for book selection is your own child. Does he seem to love books with lots of humor? Is he crazy about books having to do with dinosaurs? Does he love books by Kevin Henkes? Just like adults, children develop preferences for certain kinds of books over others, and you should try to recognize and support these preferences. At the same time, be sure to help your child expand his horizons. For example, if your child loves storybooks but tends not to like information books, look for information books on a favorite storybook topic, such as horses or sports. If your child has been resistant to poetry but likes humor books, go for poetry that is funny, such as that by Jack Prelutsky or Shel Silverstein.

* **Consider your child's developmental level.** Newborns, who are mainly able to see contrasts, will enjoy black-and-white books, like

Tana Hoban's *White on Black* or *Black on White*. As infants develop, books with bright, bold colors will become of greater interest. Throughout infancy, books with baby faces and easily recognizable everyday objects will appeal. And though paper books are appropriate for older toddlers and preschoolers, for infants and young toddlers beginning to explore books themselves, board, vinyl, and cloth books are usually best.

* **Link reading materials to your child's experiences and concerns.** If your child is getting a haircut, look for books about the hairdresser's or barber shop. If your child has developed a fear of the dark, look for books that feature characters with the same fear. *It's Okay to Be Different* by Todd Parr is great for a child struggling with issues of difference among peers. *My Visit to the Aquarium* by Aliki is wonderful to read after a visit to the aquarium, as you and your child compare and contrast what you saw with those things included in the book. (For much more about connecting books to experiences, see Chapter 8.)

* **Read book reviews.** Some library and bookstore databases include brief reviews of books. Online booksellers, such as Amazon, also include book reviews—both from book review publications and from Amazon customers. Much like with movie reviews, there is no guarantee that you will agree with the reviewer, but this information may increase the likelihood you'll be happy with the books you choose.

* **Ask friends and teachers for recommendations.** If you're like us, you consult with friends on all sorts of things. Where do their children take dance? What local restaurants have they found to be family-friendly? What day trip destinations do they like? Add asking for book recommendations to this list. Check in periodically to ask whether they've read any great children's books lately or whether they can suggest any books they think your child would like. If your child attends day care or preschool, ask his teachers for suggestions as well. One center we know includes a list of the selections they recommend with the book club order form each month. If your child's care setting doesn't do this, you might consider requesting it.

* **Use your local librarian or bookseller.** Children's librarians and booksellers spend much of their time looking at, hearing about, and selecting children's books. They can be a terrific resource for recommending books or helping you locate books on a particular topic, of a particular type, and so on. In most cases, they are happy to share their often-underutilized expertise.

* **Give it a test drive.** Whenever possible, read the book through at least once with your child to see how you, and your child, respond to it. We have avoided a number of lemons using this approach. We have found it is especially helpful when the child is really eager to purchase a book that does not look good to you. Several times, Nell's daughter was dying to have a particular mass-market book until Nell read it to her—and she quickly changed her mind!

* **Take it back.** If you realize you have made a mistake, and your child hasn't already rendered it "used," consider returning the book to the store and exchanging it for another title. You might have better luck next time!

Materials for Reading

There are millions of wonderful things for children to read—some may be quite obvious to you, and others may not. Here are some ideas from A to Z.

A: Alphabet and Other Concept Books

Alphabet books are great for building alphabet knowledge and many other aspects of literacy. And there are many wonderful alphabet books. See Chapter 6 for a list and suggestions for using them. Read books for other concepts as well—numbers, shapes, colors, and more. Hervé Tullet's *Press Here* is a great interactive book we love. There are hundreds of terrific titles to choose from and lots your child can learn.

Erin Hoey Lindstrom

B: Board Books

For infants and toddlers, board books—that is, books with rigid, unbendable pages—are a must. These books can stand up to most assaults from young children and are just fine for older children as well. The selection of board books available has grown a great deal, and you can now find many children's classics and new titles in board book format.

Board books are popular with infants and toddlers.

C: Computers and Tablets

The National Association for the Education of Young Children has taken the position that computers can be beneficial to young children if used in thoughtful, developmentally appropriate ways.[25] We agree. And lots of wonderful reading material is available digitally— e-storybooks, electronic encyclopedias, and more. There is also lots of junk available, so be sure to choose carefully. *Children's Technology Review* (childrenssoftware.com) is a valuable resource, as are early childhood educators you may know.

D: Directions

Reading directions is something most of us do almost every day and demonstrating it is a great way to show children that reading can be helpful. Make sure to read all or part of some directions out loud to your child. She may be especially interested in directions for things closely related to her, such as directions for putting together a toy or getting to a friend's house. For a discussion of directions in games, see Chapter 5.

E: E-Mail and Other Digital Texts

We know many young children who enjoy hearing e-mail messages, text messages, or other electronic texts. With your help, children can correspond with family and friends far away or use e-mail to make plans with friends nearby. Many children's book authors also have e-mail addresses publicized online, as do politicians, celebrities, and other noteworthy people. We have even e-mailed Santa Claus using an online template!

The Three Little Pigs comes alive in the hands of
young children using a flannel board and props.

F: Flannel Boards

Flannel boards are large felt surfaces on which flannel pieces can be
stuck and unstuck. Flannel board sets are available for retelling stories
such as *Goldilocks and the Three Bears.* You read the story one or more
times and then invite your child to act out the story using flannel pieces
that depict Goldilocks, each of the three bears, the chairs, the bowls of
porridge, and so on. Flannel board sets are available from sources such as
TeachChildren.com or Quill.com, or if you are really ambitious, you can
make your own. Susan made one by sliding a piece of cardboard into an
old flannel pillowcase.

G: Guides

We have found that guides to a zoo, a park, a museum, and so on are
great reading materials for children. Many children enjoy making
connections between what they are seeing in the guide and what they
will see, are seeing, or have seen at the actual location. Children also
like helping you navigate with the guide. Guidebooks to a city or other
location you are visiting also appeal to young ones.

H: How-To Books

How-to books tell children how to make or do something. There are how-to books for crafts, games, room decoration, cooking, and many more activities. Many of these books are too difficult for young children to understand and follow on their own, but some are designed for younger children. If not, you can still use them, providing lots of support. Of course, it makes little sense to read how-to books unless you are actually going to try to do the thing described, so get ready not only to read but to *do*.

I: Informative/Explanatory Texts

Informative/explanatory texts convey information about the natural or social world—for example telling about frogs or Mexico, how the body works, or where food comes from. Some people worry that these kinds of texts are too difficult for young children, but considerable research suggests that is not the case.[26] There are information books designed for even very young children, on countless topics of special interest to them. Be aware, information books for young children can be difficult to track down in libraries and bookstores. Sometimes they are intermingled with the picture books; other times they're integrated into the nonfiction section. But don't let this discourage you—they are worth the search!

Collaborative Productions

J: Junk Mail

Does junk mail drive you crazy? Hand it over to your child—she will likely love it! Many children are very curious about junk mail—What is it? Why did the sender send it? What does it say? These are fine opportunities for you to do a little selective reading aloud and a lot of explaining. Then let your child play with the mail. She may use it for all kinds of pretend play, from mail carrier to office aide to mommy or daddy. If you are still buried in mail, schools often welcome junk mail for use in their projects and pretend play as well. (See Chapter 6 for more information on Dramatic Play.)

The kitchen fridge isn't the only place where children can play with magnetic letters. Washing machines and dryers work well too—and keep those little hands busy while you work!

K: Kitchen Magnets

You may remember the magnetic poetry fad from a while back. From a literacy perspective, that is one fad that never should have faded. Children are likely to enjoy and benefit from playing with magnets and working with you to create poems, funny sayings, and other texts. The original magnetic poetry set may work, but you might also look for ones designed specifically for younger children, with larger tiles containing words that are more common and accessible (though ideally some words should be new to your child). See magneticpoetry.com for several kits for kids. Alphabet magnets are great, too!

L: Library Books

One of the most taken-for-granted assets in our country are our libraries. Libraries provide access to more material than we could read in a lifetime; they offer books on a vast array of subjects; and they're staffed with knowledgeable people to help you sort through the riches—all for free! Help your child develop a lifelong habit by taking her to the library regularly and making library books and other materials a regular part of her reading diet. For more on visiting the library, see Chapter 8.

M: Magazines

Magazine reading is popular for adults, but often overlooked for children. Yet children, like adults, often love the format, freshness, and content of magazines. There are many magazines for young children—from *Babybug*, a board-book literary magazine for infants and toddlers to *Big Backyard*, a National Wildlife Federation magazine for preschoolers. And magazine subscriptions make great gifts— they're the gift that keeps on giving!

N: Novelty Books

Let's face it, there are times when kids want a little jazzing up in their books. Books that pop up or play music, that include puzzles or rattles, that come with necklaces or stickers, that include figurines or pipe cleaners, or whatever the enhancement, are appealing to many children. We wouldn't want these to be the only books a child has, but they can be a valued part of his collection.

O: Out-and-About Books

Whenever possible, we make connections between children's experiences and books we read to them. In Chapter 8, we discuss many ways to connect books with out-and-about experiences, from running errands to taking vacations.

P: Poems

Yes, young children can appreciate this art form if given the opportunity. Children may enjoy poems about topics close to home (as in *Mommy Poems*, a collection compiled by John Micklos, Jr.), poetry about adventures, poems to make them laugh, poems to make them think, and more. There are also books based on songs that are also poems, such as *Over in the Meadow* by Ezra Jack Keats. If your child's book collection is weak on poetry, as many are, set a goal of acquiring three new books of poetry over the next year. We think you'll be glad you did!

Q: Quiz Books, Cards, and Machines

Many texts ask questions or offer brainteasers that children love to solve, such as "What number do you get when you add your ears and your eyes?"[27] Amanda Leslie's *Do Crocodiles Moo?* asks silly questions children love to answer! Quiz cards and electronic quiz machines often ask preschoolers trivia or world-knowledge questions. If your child enjoys being quizzed, include items like these in his reading material, though be sure he can answer enough questions correctly to feel good about the experience.

R: Recipes and Cookbooks

Cooking is a rich activity to engage in with children, and one with many possibilities for literacy. Family recipes are wonderful to share with children because of the history that often goes with them, but there are great cookbooks to consider as well. For suggestions and ideas about reading and cooking, see Chapter 4.

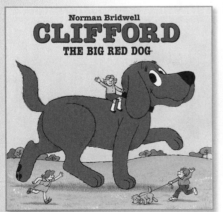

S: Storybooks

We could not forget storybooks! *Where the Wild Things Are* by Maurice Sendak, *The Cat in the Hat* by Dr. Seuss, *Clifford the Big Red Dog* by Norman Bridwell—some children's storybooks have been so loved for so long that they have become a part of our culture. For many, hearing beloved storybooks is one of the most memorable parts of childhood. So make sure storybooks are a part of your child's daily experience.

T: Touch-and-Feel Books

Many infants and young toddlers love touch-and-feel books. *Pat the Bunny* by Dorothy Kunhardt is the best-known such book, but there are now hundreds more. Some of our favorites include Dorling Kindersley's Touch and Feel series, Matthew Van Fleet's *Fuzzy Yellow Ducklings*, and the book *Feely Bugs to Touch and Feel* by David A. Carter.

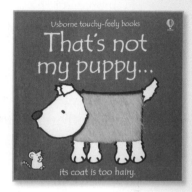

U: Use-Up Books

Sometimes the right book is a "consumable" book, or a book that children can write in—a book of mazes or puzzles, a book that allows your child to contribute to the story, and so on. Interestingly, while we often think of such books as being useless once they are used up, we have found many children like to keep and refer back to them.

V: Vinyl Books

A number of publishers make books out of vinyl or other plastics. These books work very well in the bathtub or anywhere your drooling darling might be.

W: Websites

The Internet has many sites aimed at young children. Some, such as pbskids.org, include material that appeals to nearly any child. Others appeal to only some children. For example, a lot of girls are fans of My Little Pony (hasbro.com/mylittlepony). We also read and explain material from sites not intended specifically for children if the site answers a question one of our children has asked, if it provides information about a trip we are about to take, or if it is otherwise relevant to our children's lives. If your child asks a question for which you don't have the answer—such as "What is the difference between a dolphin and a porpoise?"—

look up the answer online with your child. He or she may like the opportunity to type in the search terms himself as you spell them aloud, which provides great practice in letter recognition. Encourage your child to appreciate the richness of the Web, but as you explore, help your child begin to become a critical consumer of the material found there.

X: Maps and Other Reference Materials

X marks the spot! Many children enjoy browsing maps, seeing where they or others live, following the route as they fly or ride in a car (consider highlighting it ahead of time), and even simply folding maps back up. Other reference materials are valuable, too—when a word arises that your child does not know, when you need help explaining a concept, when a photo would help your child to understand, or when your child wants to know a fact, such as how many people live in China, consult a reference book or electronic resource. In addition to showing how to locate the information you need, you provide a great model for how to use text to answer questions about the world.

Ellen Daugherty Durr

Y: You-Make-It-Yourself Books

Some of the most treasured reading materials for many families are items they have made themselves—scrapbooks, albums, books you and your child have created together, and so on. (See descriptions of self-made alphabet books in Chapter 6 and self-made books about experiences in Chapter 8.) If you make these books available to your child for read-aloud and browsing, you will likely find her going to them over and over again. (If you are concerned about wear and tear, have the books laminated at a local copy shop.)

After hearing "Little Bunny Foo Foo," this 4-year-old decided to make a book based on the song.

Z: Zany Books

Many young children love books that are a little zany—where spaghetti ends up on a character's head, where toasters talk, where things wind up upside-down, backwards, or otherwise mixed up. Much as we want to be sure young children are exposed to serious, quality literature, we also let some silly, wacky, and not-so-serious books into the fold, as these are very often popular with children (and sometimes their parents, too!).

Don't be concerned if you don't own materials in all of these categories. Having just some can help your child, and having more is something to work toward. And this need not cost you a fortune. A number of the materials on the list come at no or very low cost (for example, directions, junk mail, and recipes), and there are even ways to get books at low or no cost. (See Finding Great Books When You Don't Have a Great Budget on the next page.)

Finding Great Books When You Don't Have a Great Budget

Here are some tried-and-true ways to fill your home with books:

* **Let friends and family members with older children know that you would love to have any books their children have outgrown.** They may appreciate the opportunity to pare down for a good cause, and to show your appreciation, you might purchase one book appropriate to the older child's age to give to the family as a thank you.

* **Check out yard sales and thrift shops.** We have gotten wonderful, high-quality hardcover and softcover books at these sites for pennies on the dollar. Expect to go often and be picky, though, because these sites have more than their share of crummy books, too.

* **Ask for books as gifts.** When people ask you what your child would like for an upcoming holiday, consider asking for books, especially in the infant and toddler years.

Raymond Coutu

* **Join a book club.** These clubs can be a good source for children's books,

A used book sale is a great way to build your child's library, and it can raise money for a good cause.

and you can get great deals if you read the fine print and keep on top of them.

* **Look for bargains at bookstores.** Many bookstores have bargain areas where you can find great deals on books that have not sold. Though, again, be selective—some of these books have not sold for good reason!

* **Inquire about frequent buyer clubs and other discounts at bookstores.** Discounts may be available for educators (which is usually broadly defined, so even if your teaching is confined to Sunday school or coaching, you may qualify) or grandparents (in which case you might ask Grandma to buy some of those books for you) or others.

* **Set up book swaps.** Consider asking a friend with a child roughly the same age to swap 10 or 20 books with you for a few weeks.

* **Use your library!** The best advice we can give you for finding great books when you don't have a great budget is to take advantage of your public library. Even small libraries have many more books than most homes do, which means lots of potential books for your family.

Looking for Books to Read to Your Child? Try These!

Eight Great Read-Alouds for Infants

Baby Animal Kisses
by B. Saltzberg

Baby Food
by M. Miller

Blue Hat, Green Hat
by S. Boynton

Mr. Brown Can Moo! Can You? Dr. Seuss's Book of Wonderful Noises
by Dr. Seuss

Playtime Peekaboo!
DK Publishing

Tomie's Little Mother Goose
by T. De Paola

The Very Busy Spider
by E. Carle

Where Is Baby's Belly Button?
by K. Katz

Eight Great Read-Alouds for Toddlers

Are Lemons Blue?
DK Publishing

Five Little Monkeys Jumping on the Bed
by E. Christelow

Freight Train
by D. Crews

Hippos Go Berserk!
by S. Boynton

Jamberry
by B. Degen

The Little Red Hen
by B. Barton

One Duck Stuck: A Mucky Ducky Counting Book
by P. Root

The Snowy Day
by E. J. Keats

Eight Great Read-Alouds for Younger Preschoolers

Corduroy
by D. Freeman

Harold and the Purple Crayon
by C. Johnson

If You Give a Pig a Pancake
by L. Numeroff

Knuffle Bunny: A Cautionary Tale
by M. Willems

The Monster at the End of This Book
by J. Stone

Swimmy
by L. Lionni

The Three Bears
by P. Galdone

Wonderful Worms
by L. Glaser

Eight Great Read-Alouds for Older Preschoolers

Actual Size
by S. Jenkins

The Family Book
by T. Parr

Fancy Nancy
by J. O'Connor

Piggie Pie
by M. Palatini

What Do You Do With a Tail Like This?
by S. Jenkins and R. Page

The Wing on a Flea: A Book About Shapes
by E. Emberley

Owen
by K. Henkes

The Seven Silly Eaters
by M. A. Hoberman

For more suggestions, try Raisingreaders.org. They have downloadable literacy kits with activities to go with more than 50 titles.

Finding Time for Nursery Rhymes

When you think of young children's literature, one thing that likely to comes to mind is Mother Goose and nursery rhymes. A number of parents we know wonder about nursery rhymes because many don't reflect the world in which children live today and may even expose children to ideas and images parents don't support. On the other hand, those parents don't want to deprive their children of material that is so often referenced in popular and literary culture.

Our position is that you should try to include some nursery rhymes among your child's reading materials, especially the more commonly referenced ones such as "Hey Diddle Diddle" or "Little Miss Muffet," and you should feel free to skip those that send questionable messages. You should also consider using versions of nursery rhymes that set them in a more modern, meaningful context. For example, *The Neighborhood Mother Goose* by Nina Crews helps children understand the rhymes by placing characters in familiar, urban settings. Kady MacDonald Denton's *A Child's Treasury of Nursery Rhymes* offers up old favorites as well as rhymes from many cultures.

You can use nursery rhymes to help your child develop his rhyming ability. For example, you might have him memorize and identify rhyming words or insert his own rhyming words. Many preschoolers love to make silly versions of well-known rhymes. For example, they might substitute /r/ for the first sound in each word in "Little Miss Muffet":

> **Rittle Riss Ruffet**
>
> **Rat ron rer ruffet**
>
> **Reating rer rerds rand rhey**
>
> **Ralong rame a rider**
>
> **Rand rat rown reside rer**
>
> **Rand rightened Riss Ruffet raway!**

Imagine how funny many children find this. Be creative, knowing that you're building your child's phonological awareness. (For much more about phonological awareness, see Chapter 5.) Give children lots of opportunities to practice these rhymes in a no-pressure, fun atmosphere.

Books for Children Who Are Beginning to Read Conventionally

yellow **frog**   blue **bird**

As discussed in Chapter 1, most children will not be reading conventionally (although they might be gleefully "pretending to read") before kindergarten. However, some will. If you have a younger child who wants to try reading conventionally, look for books with these features:

Strong picture support. Some books give strong clues to the words on the page through the illustrations or photographs. Early on, children may use these pictures to help identify the words. Over time, you should encourage your child to use the letters in the words as well. For example, if your child says "blue parrot" while reading the excerpt at right from *Rainforest Colors*, you might say, "Yes, that is a parrot, but let's look at the second word. It starts with a *b* or /b/ sound—what could the word be?"

Predictable sentence patterns. Some books use the same language pattern on each page. So once you read the title and a page or two, the child may be able to take over from there. For example, in the book *It's a Party* by Daniel Moreton and Samantha Berger, the text begins: "You're invited. / It's a pizza party." Once you read that, the child may figure out that the next page says, "It's a tea party," the next page, "It's a costume party," and so on. Over time, aim for books that are less predictable, so children need to attend more to the letters in words.

Highly familiar content. Books with the lyrics to favorite rhymes or songs, and books on topics children know a lot about, can also provide needed support to beginning readers.

Repeatedly read books. Books you have read to the child many times before are often great for them to use to practice reading themselves. Don't worry if they have "memorized" many of the words—many children who eventually become good readers start by reading mostly memorized text.

Common letter-sound relationships. Some books for young children are deliberately written to include only, or almost only, short words that use very common letter-sound patterns. For example, such books would likely include words like *cat*, *hop*, and *dig*, and would avoid words like *feline*, *leap*, and *shovel*. For young children just figuring out how to "sound out" words, such books can be helpful. But here's a tip: Make sure the text in these books still sounds somewhat natural and makes sense.

No matter how interested your child is in these kinds of books, make sure you continue to read to her as well. The higher-level language, content, and other aspects of books you read aloud continue to be very important for other aspects of her literacy development.

Spaces for Books and Reading

As adults, whether we manage to pursue our hobbies depends in large part on whether we have space and materials set aside for them. Nell seems to find many more spare moments to work on her scrapbooking when the materials are out and a table is set aside for her work. When those things aren't present, months can pass without any attention given to that hobby. Reading for pleasure can work the same way. Having reading materials readily available, and a space set aside for reading, can make a big difference in how much time you and your child spend reading.

Place Books Within Reach, Throughout the Home

One of the most common mistakes we see is tucking the child's books away in a bookcase in the bedroom. This means that these books are out of children's sight much of the time, and thus probably out of mind, too. So despite the fact that you may have a home base for books, such as shelves in the child's bedroom, consider keeping a smaller group of children's books and other reading materials in other locations in the house—

David Ammer

on the coffee table, in a basket in the kitchen, in the basement or playroom, even in the bathroom. (See Chapter 7, Literacy in Unexpected Places.) Rotate the books regularly to keep your child's interest and so that your child is exposed to books she hasn't seen in a while as well as to old favorites.

Also you may want to rethink the way you shelve books. Although the traditional spines-out method may look the neatest, it probably is not the best strategy for grabbing your child's attention. Research in schools suggests that children gravitate toward books that are displayed[28], so have at least some books with the covers facing out (and, of course, rotate which covers face out over time). Consider putting the books into crates, so that your child can see the covers easily as he selects a book. Also, consider organizing the books in some way. If you have a large collection of books, this could make it much easier to find the book you or your child is looking for. For example, you might keep all of your seasonal books in one spot, all of your information books in another, and so on.

Shannon Poynter

Look for comfortable spaces for a book nook. **Tameka Billinglea created a cozy corner for her young readers under the stairs.**

Create a Cozy Place to Read

Much as we advocate having books and other reading materials throughout the house, it is also nice to have one or more special places for reading. These are areas you create with your child that are especially cozy and comfortable. For example, you may have a big, stuffed pillow or rocking chair on which you like to read with your child. Your child may love to curl up and read with you in bed. We even know a child whose favorite reading spot is inside a play tent! The furniture in this spot doesn't have to be expensive or new—just make sure you and your child are at ease there.

Alison Billman

Materials for Drawing and Writing

Have you ever found yourself doodling just because you had a pen and paper in front of you, or writing a letter because some hotel stationery was nearby? These are more examples of how having materials around can influence literate behavior. Simply having materials for drawing and writing around your child will result in your child doing more drawing and writing. Consider making the following materials available.

A Variety of Writing Instruments

As you know, there are loads of different things with which we can write, including pens, pencils, colored pencils, markers, highlighters, crayons, chalk, charcoal, and paints. Keep your eyes out for interesting drawing and writing instruments, or ask for them for holiday gifts. You'll be surprised how much interest in drawing and writing you can generate just by introducing a new instrument. For example, a new package of Smelly Markers (markers with ink that has a scent related to the color; the red marker smells like cherry, the black smells like licorice, the yellow smells like lemon, and so on) is sure to inspire lots of marking! Rotate materials, new and old, in different parts of your house.

A Variety of Paper

Just as varying writing utensils generates interest, so too will varying papers and other materials for writing and drawing. Keep your eyes out for interesting pads of paper—pads in the shape of an animal, for example, or ones with unique colors, patterns, or textures. Look for single pieces of paper children may enjoy—a form from a local business, scrap paper from your printer, glossy paper from a magazine. Cut the fronts off greeting cards so children can write and draw on the backs (as well as study the image on the front). Look for overstock papers at local copy and print shops.

Dry-Erase Boards and Chalkboards

Consider purchasing a dry-erase board or chalkboard. Many children love to write and draw on these, and they save more than a few trees! Some companies, such as Alex, make dry-erase boards and markers that fit young children's laps and are designed for travel. Nell's daughter loved this type of dry-erase board so much she went through two of them in two years!

Shannon Poynter

Tools for writing can include classics like chalk and chalkboards and dry-erase boards and markers, or trendier tools such as gel pens, gel boards, and different-shaped pencils.

No-Mess Materials

Of course, there are times and places where a box of markers would be a recipe for disaster! And there are some children who find the walls and furniture to be far better canvases than paper. So make use of no-mess materials. Magnetic drawing boards, magic slates, magnetic words, pictures, and alphabet letters, gel boards, and similar items pose no risk for mess. Crayola also makes a line of markers, called Color Wonder®, that only work on special paper.

When used thoughtfully, computers can provide literacy-learning opportunities for young children.

Collaborative Productions

Computers

Computers can be a wonderful tool for writing. Many children, especially those with fine motor challenges, find it liberating to be able to write without physically taking pen to paper—and they love the fact that their finished pieces look so polished and "grown up." There are many computer programs that provide opportunities for children to write and illustrate their work. One we especially like is *Makiev Kid Pix 3D*. You should select software with care, and be sure to give your child lots of support as she attempts to work with this complex device. In addition, touch screens on tablets and smartphones can become your child's writing pad or sketchbook. An app such as Doodle Buddy allows little fingers to create their own lines, objects, and scribbles in many different colors and using different tools (e.g., chalk, paint brush). It also offers premade stamps and backgrounds to add to the creation.

Manipulatives

As with computers, manipulatives such as letter stamps, magnetic letters, and alphabet blocks are great as they do not require children to form letters by hand. Manipulatives can be moved around easily, enabling children to try their hand at identifying letters, letter sounds, and spelling.

Craft Supplies

You will increase drawing and writing time, as well as provide artistic experiences that are valuable in their own right, by making a variety of craft supplies available beyond what we have already recommended—glue, tape, scissors, scraps of paper and fabric, stickers, string, pipe cleaners, clay, play dough, feathers, beads, glitter, confetti, wood scraps, toilet paper and paper towel tubes, tissue paper, craft sticks, and so on. If you have a craft store in your area, wander down the aisles and familiarize yourself with the variety of materials children can enjoy. You'll be amazed. And ask around to find out if your community has a scrap-box store—a store that sells excess materials from local businesses and factories, such as tubing, textured paper, and packing materials for use as craft supplies. Shopping at scrap-box stores is not only an economical way to find a variety of supplies, it's also a great way to "reduce, reuse, and recycle."

Use Your Child's Name to Build Literacy

Children's names are often one of the first words they recognize, and children are more likely to recognize and write letters in their name than any other letters.[29] So make sure you provide lots of opportunities for your child to see his name, especially if he does not attend child care or preschool (where his name is likely to be in several places). There are many ways to do this, from labeling your child's belongings and artwork to buying personalized things like pens, barrettes, puzzles, and stools to working with your child to create a name sign for his room. As your child develops, help him write his name—perhaps just the first letter to start, and adding more letters over time. Of course, at this stage you need not worry if the writing is legible or neat. And you should never push your child to practice writing his name. Create opportunities for your child to want to write his name and, over time, this skill will develop.

David Armer

Your child's name is probably not the only name important to her. In your house, *m* might be for cousins Michael and Mercedes, *g* might be known as Grandma's letter, and best friend Sarah might have a lock on *s*. These associations are great ways to build children's knowledge of letters and the sounds associated with them.

Electronic Media and Young Children

There has been an explosion of electronic media and products made for young children. Determining which are appropriate for your child can feel overwhelming. A new product may claim to teach the letters of the alphabet or even how to read, but rarely is there research to back up such claims. In general, time with electronic media should be in moderation, and the quality should be high. As NAEYC and the Fred Rogers Center recommend, we should select interactive media that "facilitate active and creative use by young children and… encourage social engagement with other children and adults."[30] Following are some guidelines.

Crunch, crunch, crunch!
The caterpillar eats and eats.

E-Books

Good e-books can help children understand 1) what new words mean, 2) the story or topic involved, and 3) how print works. They can also help children notice sounds in words.[31] Sometimes for free but often for a fee, e-books can be downloaded or streamed on a computer or through an e-reader (e.g., Kindle, Nook, etc.). You can also buy and acccess e-books through apps, such as Scholastic's Storia app, Reading Rainbow's app, or the Sesame Street e-book app. Libraries are also good resources for e-books as they often have a subscription to services like OverDrive, and schools may have access to TumbleBookLibrary or Scholastic's Bookflix.

E-books vary in their form and features. The most basic e-book looks just like the book on paper, such as Beatrix Potter's *The Tale of Peter Rabbit* (available for free download through Project Gutenberg; http://www.gutenberg.org/ebooks/14838). This type of e-book allows you to swipe your finger to move from one page to the next.

Others have more interactive features, such as moving images, narration, sound effects, and/or a musical soundtrack; the words may appear one at a time and may be highlighted as a narrator reads them. For example, the app version of Jon Stone's *The Monster at the End of This Book* includes the voice of Grover narrating and each word is highlighted as he reads.

Interactive features are appealing, but they do not guarantee learning. In fact, some features can distract a child from important information and reduce comprehension.[32] Here are features to look for:

* **Control over images, sound, and actions,** such as controlling page turns and locations to read
* **A focus on print**, including words appearing one at a time and/or being highlighted as read
* **A focus on the main story or topic:**
  ◇ "Hotspots" that help the reader understand the story or topic better (e.g., clickable words that provide kid-friendly definitions).
  ◇ Games that are separate from the main text, such as those accessed through the main menu rather than from within the book. Games should offer your child a chance to revisit parts of the text or provide additional information related to the book.

Apps

Apps are another useful electronic product. Some apps are effectively flashcards and worksheets in an electronic form (e.g., Teach Me Toddler), some are like video games (e.g., Angry Birds), and others provide more open-ended activities (e.g., Doodle Buddy). Currently, very little is known about what and how children might learn from apps, and there are few guides to help families.[33] Therefore, we must proceed with caution and rely on our general knowledge of children and media (see pp. 120–127). Apps that allow children to explore new ideas, create and express their thoughts and feelings, and teach them how to problem solve seem more appropriate than those that merely drill skills.

Buyer Beware! Toys, Games, and Other Products Designed to "Teach" Reading and Writing

You may be wondering about materials that are specifically designed to teach children to read and write—phonics programs, kits, electronic devices, flash cards, workbooks, computer games, and the like. In general, we encourage you to avoid these products. Many of them are of poor quality, not reflecting research or best practice in literacy education. Most are not appropriate for children birth to age 5—in their design and format, and in their purposes. (Recall from Chapter 1 that although some children will be reading and writing fluently by age 5, most won't, and it should not be something you push for.)

Jaime Puccioni

That said, you may find your child asking for a product she's seen in a store or at a friend's house, or you may have read or heard about a product that sounds good to you. If you are considering purchasing the item, examine it carefully if possible and give your child a chance to try it out. Then ask yourself these questions:

* Does my child really enjoy it?

* Would my child enjoy something else more?

* Does my child feel successful at it?

* Does it teach something that seems to be an appropriate "next step" for my child?

* Might there be another product or activity that would do the same thing or better?

* Are there any dangers associated with it?

You may be surprised by that last question—but recall from the section Should I Teach My Child to Read Before Kindergarten?, in Chapter 1, that when an activity is too difficult, children can develop bad habits as a result. We don't want to purchase products that could lead to that!

Edible Writing and Drawing Materials. Some children enjoy composing with alphabet soup, alphabet cookies, or similar products. For more ideas about writing and drawing in the kitchen, please see Chapter 4.

Infant-and-Toddler-Safe Materials. Infants and toddlers should have opportunities to write and draw, too, but you have to be more careful about the materials you use with them. In addition to being nontoxic, the materials should not pose a choking hazard or the less worrisome but still considerable hazard of ruining

From scissors to string to scrap paper, a variety of tools and materials is important in encouraging young artists to express themselves.

your walls or furniture. Some paints fit this bill, as do some markers. A number of materials you might use in the bathtub, such as foams, allow for drawing and writing there. Some of the no-mess materials discussed earlier in the chapter also work for infants and toddlers. As with most things, you will have to use common sense as well as knowledge of your child to make appropriate choices about writing and drawing materials.

Of course, as with books, it is important to make these materials available not just in one place, but throughout the home. This greatly increases the chances that your child will draw and write every day.

Concluding Thoughts

There is probably some aspect of your home in which you take great care—perhaps it's the décor or the garden, or the organization or cleanliness. It is well worth your while to take such care with the literacy environment of your home as well. This will go such a long way toward encouraging interactions with print throughout the day and throughout the year. For your family, make sure home is where the print is.

WRITING MATERIALS

CHAPTER 4

In the Kitchen

Pamela Green

Your kitchen is probably one of the busiest places in your home, morning, noon, and evening. You prepare for the day there, your children prepare for school or child care, someone cooks the meals, someone sorts the mail, someone makes a shopping list, and so forth. Amid this bustle, literacy and language use is happening full throttle, so how can you make the most of it? At the kitchen table, while your family catches up on daily events, your child can be gaining valuable oral language skills. When he watches and helps you follow a recipe, he will be engaging with print and seeing how useful it is. And as he undertakes messy painting projects you reserve for the kitchen, he will be experiencing art and literacy at the same time.

In this chapter, we discuss oral language development (as the kitchen is a great place to promote that development), and general literacy development through cooking, art, and writing, which can happen throughout the day.

Beyond "Baby Talk": Children's Oral Language Development

The higher-pitched voice, the short phrases, the slow rhythm, the exaggerated arm and facial movements: You would get a strange look if you used "parentese" with another adult, but it seems perfectly natural when you use it with infants and very young children.[34] What we do when we talk with young children has a big impact on their own language development.

Oral language develops at an amazing rate from a child's earliest days. And anyone who has heard a toddler use "adult" words—in the right context, no less—knows that oral language also develops in remarkable ways. Consider that by the age of 18 months, "most children can pronounce four-fifths of the English phonemes and use 9 to 20 words" and, between their second and third birthdays, toddlers' vocabularies expand from 300 to 1,000 words![35] So with each new day, young children's language skills are broadening. It's delightful to us as observers and essential for the children who experience it.

Early Language Development, Birthday by Birthday

In this section, we list just some of the language milestones young children typically achieve. Be aware that these milestones, based on information from the American Speech-Language-Hearing Association, provide *general guidelines* for what to expect from one year to the next. As you read them, it's important to keep in mind that children develop at different rates. For example, some children utter their first words at 8 months whereas others do so around 12 months. Differences between your child and other children in language development are normal. But having a general sense of what's to come can help you think about and promote your child's language development, wherever she is and wherever she is headed. If you are concerned that your child may be significantly delayed in reaching these milestones, consult your pediatrician or a certified speech-language pathologist.

Before their first birthday, babies:

* Startle when they hear loud noises, and turn to look in the direction of sounds.

* Often smile or quiet down when people speak to them, and learn to recognize caregiver's voices.

* Love music and games like peek-a-boo.

* Communicate needs and wants initially by crying differently for different needs.

* Make cooing noises, which later transitions into babbling.

* Start to make speech sounds in the second half of the first year, often uttering first words between eight and twelve months of age.

* Start following simple requests, showing that they know some words.

After their first birthday and before their second, babies:

* Point to pictures, items, and body parts when named.

* Show increasing comprehension of simple requests and questions.

* Understand and produce new words every month.

* Begin uttering two-word statements or questions, such as "more milk," or "where Daddy?"

After their second birthday and before their third, toddlers:

* Start following more complex requests and showing increasing conceptual understanding (for example, contrasts between *big* and *little* or *up* and *down*).

* Enjoy listening to stories for increasing periods.

* Have words for almost everything and use these words to ask questions or to shift conversation towards objects.

* Can be understood by most people who have regular contact with them, although strangers may not understand their speech.

* Enjoy wordplay, such as rhyming.

ORAL LANGUAGE

After their third birthday and before their fourth, preschoolers:

* Answer simple questions and retell.

* Often speak smoothly in sentences of four or more words and can usually be understood by anyone.

* Use corrective self-talk, such as repeating something that they're not supposed to do. (For example, a small child at a store might mutter to herself, "No. Don't touch. No. Don't touch.")

After their fourth birthday and before their fifth, preschoolers:

* Are able to communicate comfortably with both children and adults.

* Can answer simple questions about stories, and when they tell a story it is likely to stay on topic.

* Provide lots of details when they speak.

* Identify and repeat rhyming words.

* Pronounce most sounds correctly, though may still struggle with some sounds, such as *l, s, r, v, z, ch, sh, th.*

* Use grammar resembling that used by adults, although they will still use some forms not used by adults. (For example a 4-year-old might say, "I goed up the stairs.")

After their fifth birthday, children:

* Have mastered a wide array of pronunciations.

* Are well on their way to becoming sophisticated speakers, with an ever-growing bank of vocabulary and increasingly complex syntax.[36]

What Can You Do to Boost Oral Language?

Promoting oral language can happen through daily activities, such as those that happen in the kitchen. Just talking to your child is the first step, which, we realize, is not always easy because of life's many demands.

So here are some tips for making high-quality conversations with your child a regular part of your day.

Take Every Opportunity to Talk With Your Child

Talk about almost anything, regardless of his age and language abilities. Consider conversing about people she knows, places she will be going, and things she likes to do and see. You can also describe what you're doing while in the midst of doing it. For example, as you prepare lunch, explain what you're up to: "Let's see, we need to have some lunch. What looks good to you? Why don't we get some bread, some peanut butter, and some jelly. Mmmm, this is one of my favorite kinds of sandwich. How about you?"

Collaborative Productions

Listen to What Your Child Says

Listen as you would to a friend or colleague—let your child know that you want to hear what he has to say. If you can't devote your attention to him at that moment, say, "Just a minute—I really want to hear what you are saying" and hold your finger up until you are ready to listen or suggest your child return in a few minutes. Then make sure you get back to that conversation.

Think About the Kind of Language You Typically Use

Talk can often become reduced to commands ("Be careful," "Come here," "Clean up"), so be sure to discuss past events or events yet to come, in addition to telling stories and giving explanations. Mothers who talk beyond the here and now raise children with stronger language and literacy skills.[37]

ORAL LANGUAGE

Great Ideas for Helping Your Child Fall in Love With Words

Let's face it—as adults, we're not always curious about the most erudite topics. Many of us tend to devour news about celebrities and fashion trends and the latest vacation destinations. But what we want to promote in our children is curiosity about ideas and words. We want children to be aware of words and develop a natural interest in the variety and meaning of the multitude of words available to them. In other words, we want children to have "word consciousness."[38] Here are some ways you can help your child develop it:

* **Praise your child when he asks about a word he doesn't know.** You might say, "Good question!" or "That's great that you asked about a word you don't know."

* **Praise your child when she lets you know she doesn't understand.** You might say, "Good question!" or "I'm glad you asked about that," and then explain it so she does understand.

* **Show your own word consciousness.** You might ask, "What does that mean?" which is useful when your child uses a word you don't know (such as one he might have picked up from a television program or one that he has made up). You might also exclaim, "Isn't that a wonderful word!" or suggest, "I wonder if that's called _____ because of _____."

* **Create interest in words.** You can do this by reading books that have interesting words or word play. You can also use and introduce words that have interesting sounds and/or meaning, such as *squishy*, *platypus*, and *verbose*.

Use Interesting, Sophisticated Words

Don't be afraid to use words that your child may not know. But be sure to use them in contexts that will clue your child in to what they mean, perhaps by your facial expression or by pointing to an object. For instance, you can replace words such as *happy* and *mad* with more sophisticated words such as *delighted*, *thrilled*, and *ecstatic* or *upset*, *angry*, and *furious*. Often, your face will show just what the word means! Find occasions, too, to insert more scientific or technical words to describe something, such as labeling a cicada or monarch butterfly by its name when you and your child see one outside rather than calling it a "bug." When you do this, you should also give the child information about the larger category for the word—for example, you might say, "Look at that cicada; it's an interesting kind of insect!"

Respond to Your Child and Expand on What She Says

The extent to which a mother responds to her child is one of the best predictors of many aspects of that child's language development.[39] We suggest that this applies to fathers and other caregivers, too. Respond to gestures or verbalizations that your child offers. When she points to her sippy cup, you can elaborate on this and say, "You're pointing to your cup. Would you like some milk to drink?"

Here are other examples:

CHILD: [Points at a light on the ceiling.]

MOM: You like the light.

CHILD: [Grunts and gestures toward counter.]

MOM: You want something from here? These crackers? [Holds up crackers.] This milk? [Holds up milk.]

Also, recast what your child says. When he hears the roar of a motorcycle passing and says, "Mo go," you can recast this by saying, "Yes, that's a motorcycle! It is going down the street. It can take you places just like a car or city bus."

Here are a few more examples:

CHILD: [Holds up ball.] Ball!

DAD: You found a ball.

CHILD: Apple.

DAD: Would you like an apple?

CHILD: [Points to a photo of a dog on a book cover.] Doggie!

DAD: What a cute doggie!

CHILD: Brown.

DAD: Yes, that's a brown dog.

Engage in Language-Rich, Imaginative Play

When you engage in pretend talk with your child you are calling up things that are not real or giving real objects imaginary identities—a pencil, for example, becomes an airplane. Props may encourage this type of talk—plastic figures and some Legos may bring to life imaginary towns and townspeople or a stuffed animal may remind you both of last week's tea party. By using imagination and talk, children benefit with stronger language skills later on.[40]

In the following example, a mother and her 4-year-old child are playing with cars and using pretend talk:

CHILD: You better watch out for that guy.

MOM: I know, he's gonna pass him. Oh, he's gonna pass on the side. [Makes engine sounds.] Whoops, now he's gonna make a U-turn. [Makes more engine sounds.] Whoops, now he has to go slow. He's in back of a bus. [Makes more engine sounds.]

CHILD: How did he come back over that side?

MOM: I don't know; he's just driving around. He likes to drive.

CHILD: You—he has to drive. He's the teacher, right? He's the . . .[41]

Ask Open-Ended Questions

We often ask questions that can be answered with a simple "yes" or "no." But if we really want to boost young children's oral language, we should ask open-ended questions. Open-ended questions can't be answered in one word (such as "yes," "no," "blue," "dog," etc.); instead, they require more complex responses—and, in the process, children get practice in complex oral language. For example, instead of asking, "What is that?" you might try asking, "Can you tell me more about that?" See more examples in the chart on the next page.

How You Ask Matters

Closed Questions

	Responses
Is he a new toy or an old toy?	Old.
Who is Joe? He's the what?	Baby.
Think back in the story. They went to pick up his…	Big sister.
Do you think Nelle is going to be happy or mad?	Mad.
Somebody else had already what?	Found him.
Was she being nice to her little brother?	Yeah.

Open-Ended Questions

	Responses
How did the other kids like Stephanie's ponytail?	First they liked it when she didn't have it to her ear, and then they kept calling her ugly, and now they're gonna be jealous, real jealous.
What's going on?	George got into trouble anyway.
What's the problem with having a fawn as a pet?	'Cause he'll eat everything. He's like a goat.
Charlie looked at the girls and purred. What's that tell us?	The girls are happy that they might have found him.
Why would termites be a worry for the owl?	Because the termites might eat the owl's home cause it's made out of wood.
What happened?	The people saw the sign maker and chased him into the woods, and they thought that the sign maker did it, but the boy did.

Adapted from M. G. McKeown and Beck (2003).[42]

Janel Bennett

Redirecting children to more appropriate behavior can give us a chance to build their language and their social skills at the same time.

Tell and Explain

Is your child's favorite question "Why?" This question is actually quite legitimate: Your child is wondering why something is the way it is, why she has to do something, or why she can't do something else, among other things. Such questions introduce wonderful occasions for you to explain how things work, why we do certain things (and not other things), what led you to a particular decision, and so on. In fact, explanatory talk is another hallmark of a quality oral-language environment.[43] Parents often tell their children to do something, or not to do something, without explaining the reason *why*. By explaining to your child, for example, why she should (or shouldn't) do something, you may just satisfy that "why" question before it is even asked. Instead of simply saying, "Don't run," you can elaborate by saying, "Walk when you're near the pool. I'm concerned you might slip and fall." There are many situations in which you can offer explanations that shed light for your child. When she asks about the world around her—why the sun "goes away" at night, for example, or why giraffes have long necks—you have the perfect opportunity to develop both language and world knowledge. Don't worry if you can't answer every question posed—together, you and your child can look for answers in a book, a magazine, or on the Internet.

Sing Songs

You don't have to be a professional singer to enjoy sharing a tune with your child. In fact, songs that have rich words and rhyming can promote phonological awareness, vocabulary knowledge, and syntax (i.e., the way words are strung together). Singing, on- or off-key, can be quite an enjoyable experience for children and quite a beneficial one for their language development, too. (See Chapter 5 for more on singing songs.)

Think About Using Baby Signs

Baby signs[44] are gestures for particular words, such as *more* or *done*, words commonly heard in the kitchen. They can be an early bridge for communicating with your baby. Linda Acredolo and Susan Goodwyn are two of the main researchers working in this area, and their work over the past few decades has supported the position that baby signs can help, not hinder, oral language development,[45] which is a common concern. In addition, they report that parents who use this approach find that using baby signs reduces frustration for everyone involved because it helps very young children communicate their feelings and ideas before they can do so with words. For example, Susan Bennett-Armistead has found that her son, Ababu, learned rather quickly the signs for *more* and *food* at a time when others couldn't understand his pronunciation of those words. There is still more to learn about this relationship, and it's important to use the spoken words along with the signs.[46] Then, when your child begins to speak, help him transition from signs with speech to just using speech.

Engage in Extended Conversations

Sometimes we can go through the day and have very few extended conversations with our children. But the more often we have lengthier discussions, the better it is for them. Extended discourse promotes not only sophisticated language development but cognitive development as well. That is because talking at length about a single topic helps children look at it from many angles, integrate information across sources, make connections, and so on.

So when can you engage in extended discussions with your children? Well, anytime, really, but mealtimes are often perfect for this kind of conversation. When you converse with your child at mealtime, you ensure not only that he is taking in nutrients to help him grow physically, but also that his language and literacy skills are being nourished, so they can grow as well.

Seize Storytelling Opportunities

With all the great talking that can happen at mealtime, don't be surprised if you find yourself (and others) telling lots of stories. Stories can be fun to tell and a delight to hear, but more important for your child, story-telling can promote her language and literacy. For more on promoting storytelling, see Chapter 5.

ORAL LANGUAGE

What's Cooking? Literacy Learning Through Food Preparation

Even before you put food on the table, your child can be learning all about literacy and language in the kitchen. Whether you're preparing a gourmet meal or heating up macaroni and cheese, cooking provides a wealth of opportunities to fire up your child's desire to read and write, speak and listen, view and create.

What Can You Do to Boost Literacy Through Cooking?

Here are some ideas to get the juices flowing.

Read and Write Recipes

Invite your child to join you as you consider new or old recipes. Have him observe you reading a recipe and talking about your plan to prepare it. Invite him to stir or even dump ingredients into mixing bowls. Consider looking for easy and quick recipes for snacks and main meals. Cookbooks such as the ones listed in the box on page 86 offer loads of kid-friendly recipes. See Six Easy Snacks, on the next page, for more handy recipes. Another idea is to create with your child a cookbook of your own that contains family favorites.

David Armistead

Talk as You Cook

As you cook, talk about what you are doing. Later, help your child explain the cooking process to someone who was not there. Questions such as "What ingredients did you put in the bowl?" or "How did you help me make the banana bread?" can elicit brief, specific responses or rich, detailed accounts. Whether your child is a toddler or a 4-year-old, he can successfully retell his experience—and boost oral language skills.

Use Cooking Vocabulary

Words such as *teaspoons, tablespoons, one-half pound,* and *one-third cup* are prevalent in cooking. By introducing cooking terms, and explaining what they mean, you not only promote literacy, but also numeracy—the ability to use numbers.

Check Out Food Labels

In addition to helping you make healthy food choices, food labels provide great opportunities for children to interact with print. Researchers have found that young children can identify and remember labels on food, cleaning products, and other household items, which is a sign that children are starting to "read" print in their environment.[47]

Consult Take-Out Menus

When you have no time for cooking and decide to order take-out, consult that pile of menus you may have stored in a drawer. Choose a menu and show your child all the possible meals you could order, pointing to options that he might enjoy. Even if you aren't planning to take food out or order food using another source (such as the Internet), printed menus, with their colorful words and pictures, are interesting to most children.

Six Easy Snacks

Here are some ideas for snacks that almost all children can create. Before you prepare them, though, be sure your child is not allergic to any of the ingredients—often, tasty substitutes are available.

* **Ants-on-a-log:** Spread peanut butter on celery and sprinkle raisins on top. If your child has peanut allergies, substitute cream cheese for peanut butter.

David Ammer

* **Cheese trees:** Cut cheese into small cubes and have your child place a pretzel stick upright into them.

* **Fruit salad:** Have your child combine apples, raisins, grapes, oranges, and any other fruit of her choice—presliced to avoid cutting herself.

* **Gorp:** Have your child combine mixed cereal, dried fruit, pretzels, yogurt-covered raisins, and other healthy ingredients of her choice.

* **Mini pizzas:** Spread pizza sauce on English muffins and sprinkle with mozzarella cheese and toppings of your child's choice. Bake until cheese melts.

* **Quesadillas:** Stuff tortillas with cheese and other ingredients such as refried beans and chopped chicken. Bake or microwave until cheese melts. Cut into quarters. Your child may even enjoy dipping pieces into salsa. (Try mild first!)

Cookbooks for Kids

Cooking Art: Easy Edible Art for Young Children
by M. F. Kohl and J. Potter

Mom and Me Cookbook
by A. Karmel

Feed Me I'm Yours: Baby Food Made Easy!
by V. Lansky

Kids Cooking: A Very Slightly Messy Manual.
Klutz

With every snack and meal you make, you show by example how essential literacy is to accomplishing the many tasks we carry out each day.

From Mess to Masterpiece: Literacy Learning Through Art

Although we don't advocate doing arts-and-crafts projects only in the kitchen, they are often best carried out there, where a sink, a mop and broom, paper towels, and a trash bin are readily available. Creative expression is usually messy. In fact, we've found that often the messier it is, the more creative it is!

Reading and writing (and other aspects of emergent literacy) can easily take place while creating art. Depending on your child's age, he may be using pictures and words to express his thoughts, feelings, understandings, and stories on paper. For example, he might write his name on a painting he has just created or "read" a story to you from a picture he has just drawn.

What Can You Do to Boost Literacy Through Art?

Although art and literacy can stand on their own and serve separate purposes, they can also enhance one another when a child puts them together. Here's what you can do to make this happen.

Inspire Imagination

Here are some ways to help your little artist develop literacy as she creates her masterpieces.

Raymond Coutu

* **Focus on process rather than product.** Let your child know that there's not one right way to make something and that one of the best parts about being creative is this freedom to experiment with materials.

* **Don't model the "right way" to do something.** This sends the message that there is no room for children to explore new ways of creating.

* **Notice creativity around you.** Marvel with your child about the innovative things you see around town, on television, and in newspapers and magazines. By talking about creativity that abounds, you encourage your child to explore his own creative side.

* **Concentrate on your child's creations and avoid comparing them to other children's.** By comparing, you suggest that one child's work is better than another's. There is no faster way to extinguish creativity.

* **As tempting as it may be, avoid "helping" your child modify his work to "improve" it.** Corrections can dilute a child's meaningful experiences with art.[48] Each time you're tempted to step in, remember that artistic skills, like literacy skills, take time to develop.

* **Say something like, "Tell me about your drawing."** You'll be amazed at the amount of information your child will give you, much more than if you simply ask, "What's that?" We do not advocate asking young children what their picture is because that implies that it has to "be" something. Perhaps a child just wants to draw "purple." If so, that's okay. Furthermore, by asking her what the picture depicts, we send the subtle message "Whatever it's supposed to be, it doesn't look like it!"

Provide a Variety of Materials

Often, young children just need a pencil and some paper, and creativity starts to flow. However, sometimes that's not enough. Other materials, like the ones listed below, can spark creativity and promote literacy:

Children can have very specific purposes for their writing, so ask, "Tell me about that" or "Read this to me."

* Craft supplies such as scissors, tape, glue, fabric pieces, string, paper scraps, clay and play dough, stickers, pipe cleaners, feathers, tissue paper, and cardboard from cereal or other food boxes

* Painting and drawing supplies such as watercolors, finger paints, paintbrushes, pens, crayons, markers, chalk, colored pencils, easels, and smocks

* Papers of various shapes, colors, sizes, and textures

* Books on making crafts, such as *The Klutz Book of Paper Airplanes* by Doug Stillinger

* Sheets with guidelines for making individual crafts

* Books on artists and their work, such as *Museum ABC* by the staff at the Metropolitan Museum of Art

By talking about new and interesting materials with your child, you also encourage oral language, in addition to creative expression. New words will likely arise, such as *sticky, stringy, triangle, rough,* and *masterpiece,* which your child may begin to use on his own. And having real objects to see, smell, touch, and work with will help him understand what these new words mean. (See Chapter 3 for many more ideas on materials to inspire artwork and drawing, including no-mess materials.)

Make Your Child's Work Public

Find places to display your child's artwork—the refrigerator is one favorite spot. You can also adorn windows and doors. Sending artwork to friends and relatives provides an opportunity for learning about the power of written communication.

The refrigerator isn't the only place to display your child's artwork. Consider other creative places to display creations, such as on your child's bedroom door and on different walls around your house.

Meagan Shedd

Meagan Shedd

Meagan Shedd

Even very young children, when given appropriate materials, can engage in activities that promote writing and drawing.

David Ammer

Figure 4.1 (top): A young child creates a work of art by scribbling.

Figure 4.2 (bottom): This child portrays the important people in her life—her parents and herself.

Drawing Development: From Marks and Scribbles to People and Places

Artwork by very young children will look different from artwork by older children and adults. When you look at your infant's, toddler's, or preschooler's creations, appreciate the distinctive aspects of the work—the scribbles, the blobs, the disproportionate heads on people—for they represent much more than marks on a page. They serve as indicators of your child's emerging abilities as an artist.[49] Viktor Lowenfeld documented six stages of drawing development that occur in children between toddlerhood and adolescence.[50] The first two stages apply to ages we address in this book.

Scribbling (ages 2 to 4): Children scribble with or without guidance, and their scribbling develops over time from disordered (uncontrolled) to longitudinal (controlled, repetitive) to circular (more complex, controlled) markings. (See Figure 4.1.) As time goes on, children can usually name or tell stories about what they have drawn. However, they do not usually choose color with intention. They enjoy making large movements when they draw. . . and mark surfaces, such as walls (as you may know all too well!).

Preschematic (ages 4 to 7): During these ages, children become more representational when they draw. For example, when drawing a human figure, they might use a circle for the head and vertical lines for the legs. (See Figure 4.2.) They may not capture the space or relationship between objects or elements, but they are starting to capture the elements themselves from the world around them in their drawings. Cathy Malchiodi, director of the Institute for the Arts and Health, writes that Lowenfeld "emphasiz[es] the discovery of relationships among drawing, thinking, and reality" during this stage.[51]

Beyond Baby Scrawls: Children's Writing Development

Just as Annie's good friend Sarah was heading out the door to run errands recently, she found a note from her daughter Elaina taped to the door leading to the garage. Since Elaina was only 2½, the note was made up of scribbles, so Sarah asked Elaina to tell her about it. Elaina explained that the note said, "Mom, please remember to buy more crayons." She wrote the note and posted it on the garage door because her mother had forgotten to buy crayons the week before. In other words, Elaina had a clear and genuine purpose for writing.

Meagan Shedd

A child's request for more crayons, posted where her parents can see it

Early Writing Development

Writing, much like drawing, has been studied for many years by literacy researchers.[52] One of those researchers is Elizabeth Sulzby, who documented six stages that young children progress through to become writers of conventional text. Becoming familiar with these stages and, therefore, knowing what to expect can help you to support your child's emerging writing:[53]

* Writing through drawing
* Writing through scribbling
* Writing through letter-like forms
* Writing by familiar units or letter strings
* Writing through estimated (or temporary) spellings
* Writing through conventional spelling

The Real Story About Handwriting

Young children's handwriting isn't usually the neatest. And, as a parent, you might be concerned that your child is learning bad habits early on if she writes letters in ways that seem messy to you. However, crisp, clear handwriting before formal schooling is not something to push. Before your child enters elementary school, he should have the freedom to explore letter formations without having to worry about forming the letter z perfectly. Once he enters school, there will likely be a handwriting chart that the school or district uses, and there may be a handwriting program. In the meantime, if your child asks how to make a certain letter, demonstrate a simple construction of the letter as follows:

Be aware: These are not rigid stages; this means that your best friend's son may not progress through them in exactly the same way your son does.[54] Also, throughout the preschool years, your child may go back and forth between stages depending on what else he is thinking about and working on.

Writing Through Drawing

Whether children are trying to capture their home, grandmother, or pet—or any other subject for that matter—drawing pictures is one of the first ways they put their thoughts and ideas on paper.[55] It is one of the first ways they tell stories. This makes sense because many young children believe that we "read" the pictures in books and not the words.[56]

This is a child's documentation of dandelion seeds blowing away after a wish has been made.

Writing Through Scribbling

Between the ages of 2½ and 3 years, many children begin to recognize differences between drawing and writing. Their writing may begin to be distinguishable from their drawing; for example, while their writing may be composed of squiggly lines, their drawing may consist of circles and scribbles. Still, at this age, properties of drawing and writing are very much intermingled. Children learn to structure their scribbling to resemble text structures they know. For instance, on page 13, the first sample shows a little girl's scribbled shopping list. You can see how much the scribbles resemble an adult's typical shopping list.

Writing through scribbling

Writing Through Letter-Like Forms and Letter Strings

Following scribbling, young children begin to create letters and letter-like forms on paper to convey messages and ideas. Although these shapes are not always conventionally formed letters, they look like letters. Children may write strings of letters that do not actually compose words, but which the children may refer to as words. Letters and shapes may also be included in the strings early on, although this will diminish as children increasingly come to see letters as a separate system.

Writing through letter-like forms and letter strings

**Writing through temporary spelling:
"No one can come in except Mommy."**

Writing through conventional spelling

At this stage, children understand that writing is made up of something other than drawings and scribbles. It's made up of letters and words. This is an important milestone.

Writing Through Temporary Spelling and Conventional Spelling

During the preschool years, children's letter formations become more conventional. Children also begin to match the sounds they hear to the letters that they write, and letters begin to represent syllables in words.[57] Representing sounds in words involves temporary or invented spelling.[58] Temporary spelling is just that—children test out different ways words might be spelled as they progress toward conventional spelling. At this point, children spell words based on their knowledge of the sounds of letters and letter combinations. Many early childhood educators allow children to explore writing in this way, so don't be surprised to see this on work that is sent home, if your child spends time in child care. It's important to allow children to explore, try out, and play around with spellings in their own writing and in others' writing. In fact, this actually supports their phonological awareness development. (See Chapter 5 for more about phonological awareness.) These early years are not the time to force correct spellings of words or drill children with flash cards. They will develop spelling skills in due time and within supportive environments.

What Can You Do to Boost Literacy Through Writing?

In the kitchen, we typically write any or all of the following:

* Grocery lists

* To-do lists

* Notes to remind family members about chores ("Take out the trash, please."), upcoming events ("Don't forget soccer practice, 4:00!"), and ways to be reached ("I'm at Rosa's. Her number is 325-555-8976, in case you need me.")

* Greeting cards, birthday cards, and letters to communicate with family members and friends

* Checks to pay bills

* Labels for food containers

* Names on school- and work-related items such as lunch bags and file folders

When you carry out these activities in front of your child, you demonstrate how useful writing is. And when you invite him to join you, his own writing skills are likely to blossom. Before you know it, notes like Elaina's will begin to pop up in your kitchen.

When Should My Child Be Able to Recognize Lowercase and Uppercase Letters?

Young children typically learn uppercase alphabet letters first. According to the Common Core State Standards, your child should be able to recognize all of the letters in the alphabet, both uppercase and lowercase, by the end of kindergarten. There is even some evidence to suggest that children should be able to recognize 18 uppercase and 15 lowercase letters by the end of Pre-K.[59] Making sure that your child sees examples of letters in both forms (upper- and lowercase) will help her start to put together the fact that the letter *b* can look like this—B—or this—b. In addition, you can provide materials such as magnetic letters, wooden letters, and alphabet stamps that include upper- and lowercase letters. You can also get some models of the alphabet (such as an alphabet chart) displayed at your child's eye level in an area where she writes frequently. Finally, when your child sees you writing something during your daily activities, you can use the occasion to point out some of the upper- and lowercase letters that you're writing.

David Armistead

David Armistead

In addition to these activities, here are some other ways to encourage your child to explore writing in the kitchen.

Put a Pad of Paper and a Pencil Within Reach

When you leave these items on the counter or post them on the refrigerator, your child is more likely to use them. And messages may start to appear.

Keep a Small Supply of Writing Instruments Around

Fill a small container with some of your child's favorite writing instruments, such as markers, crayons, colored pencils, or gel pens. Place the container within your child's reach, along with a small stack of paper, and remind her to use it. While she's waiting for bread to toast, soup to cool, or her older brother to set the table, she can be composing and drawing in the kitchen.

Take Dictation

Taking dictations from your child is another option for getting her ideas, messages, and stories on paper. By taking dictation, you model how and why we write and promote some aspects of emergent literacy, such as letter-sound correspondence. It is especially useful when your child has a lot to communicate, and writing it on her own might be too frustrating—for example, if she is attempting a story or a letter to a family member or friend.

Have Your Child Create Birthday Invitations

Birthdays are a big deal, and often, birthdays mean having a party with family or friends. Birthdays also provide a great opportunity to promote writing. You can encourage your child to create invitations to a birthday dinner or birthday party. For a younger child, have him draw a picture on the front of the invitation and use other materials such as stamps, glitter, and so on to decorate. You can then write the details inside and explain what you are writing to your child. If the child is a bit older, he can not only draw and decorate the invitation but also contribute to the written message as much as possible. You can then fill in other details as needed.

Have Your Child Create Placemats

Creating placemats for everyone in the family is a great way for your child to showcase her writing and drawing. Because these placemats are used at every meal, they serve as a daily reminder that writing can be useful. They also serve as a wonderful way to show off your child's emerging talents as a writer and artist. (For even more ideas, see Chapter 3.)

Affix Magnetic Letters to the Lower Half of the Refrigerator

Magnetic letters can be very enticing to young children because they put the alphabet within reach and encourage them to create words. All this *without* the labor involved with writing by hand.

A child-created placemat picturing a doughnut factory

Concluding Thoughts

From recipe-making and mealtime conversation to art projects and writing, your kitchen can be overflowing with activities that support literacy and language development. In this chapter, we highlighted ways that you can promote your child's oral language development. We also discussed how art and literacy blend well together. And we focused on opportunities to engage your child in writing. The kitchen certainly provides the context for cooking up literacy and language in creative, enjoyable ways.

WRITING

CHAPTER 5

In the Living Room

David Ammer

Over the years, you've probably noticed similarities among living rooms you've visited—the couch, the coffee table, a television, perhaps some books. But these similarities mask important differences in ways families use the living room: Some families rarely find themselves together long enough to enjoy time in the living room, some use the living room only for entertaining guests, some spend hours in the living room, glued to the latest hit television programs, and so on. In this chapter we describe ways you can use your living room to build literacy as well as family togetherness. Specifically, we discuss the following activities:

* Playing games

* Giving performances

* Watching television and video

We talk about the promises and pitfalls associated with these activities. By the time you finish the chapter, you will have many ideas for things to do—and a few things not to do—in your living room to foster literacy as well as quality family time.

Playing Games

Have you heard about Hasbro's campaign to promote a "Family Game Night" in households across America? Most families we know who have tried it have been pleased with the results. Why? Games provide an opportunity for family members to come together and interact rather than everyone doing their own thing or sitting silently in front of the television. What's more, many games offer opportunities to develop literacy. Here are a few.

Games With Instructions

Any game with written instructions provides an opportunity for children to see the use of an important type of print (what some scholars call "procedural text" because it imparts the procedure for how to do something). You can read instructions aloud, taking breaks to clarify or explain. And you can consult the instructions as needed throughout the game. Your child may want to consult the directions with you—the section on the components of the game is often an especially good one to co-read with your child, as he may be able to read the numbers or even guess at the words.

Number of Players: 2 to 4

Getting Started

- Decide which game you want to play. Turn the game board to the appropriate side.
- Each player chooses a game piece and puts it on the Start space.
- To see who goes first, every player tosses one yellow cube. The player who rolls the letter closest to the beginning of the alphabet goes first.

Game 1: Capital City

Get around the city by matching the lowercase letters with their capital letters.

You Need

- Capital City game board
- 4 yellow cubes
- game piece for each player

How to Play

1. On his or her turn, a player tosses all four yellow cubes. The player looks at the letters on the cubes and on the board. He moves forward to the nearest space with a matching letter. For example, if a player at the Start space rolls an E, D, S, and U, he or she moves to the *d* space. The next player then takes a turn.

2. Players continue taking turns rolling the cubes and moving ahead to the nearest matching letter. If no cube matches the letters on any of the remaining spaces, the player cannot advance. The turn passes to the next player.

3. After a player has reached the final letter space *(xyz)*, he or she must roll a capital E, N, or D to move into the End space. The first person to reach End wins the game!

Games With Print

Many games include print on the game board or cards, if only to label the items, such as the sea creatures in many versions of Go Fish, or as the focus of the game, as with Boggle Jr. When the print is somewhat incidental to the game, as with Go Fish, take the time to read, point to, and refer to the print when playing. If the print is central, as with Boggle Jr., take advantage of this focus, but, of course, be sure your child is enjoying and feeling successful with the game. (See discussion of pushing children before they are ready, in Chapter 1.)

David Ammer

This preschooler is enjoying Boggle Jr., a game focused on print.

Games With "No Reading Required"

Many games for toddlers and preschoolers are marketed as "no reading required." This is fine, as the games can generally support development of other skills, such as counting or taking turns. But you can also turn a "no reading required" into a "reading involved" game when you think that would be enriching for children. For example, you could replace some of the color cards in Candyland with the color names written in the color, and eventually replace those with the color names written in black. Color words are often among the first that children learn to read. In many cases, words can be identified by their first letter (for example, if it starts with *g* it must be *green*), and a few require children to practice looking beyond the first letter (for example, if it starts with *p*, is it *pink* or *purple*?).

GAMES

Games Based on Books

There are games, including some with no reading required, that are based on books or characters from books. These games may inspire interest in these books or characters, and the family might enjoy a related

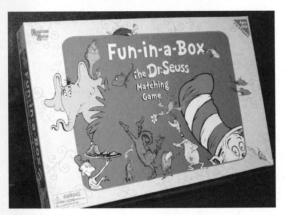

read-aloud before or after playing the game. For example, the game Fun-in-a-Box: The Dr. Seuss Matching Game focuses on the many books of Dr. Seuss. After playing, the family might choose a favorite Dr. Seuss book for a read-aloud.

Concept Games

Many games can build children's vocabulary and concept knowledge. Twenty Questions and Categories are two such games, which are described in detail on pages 167–169. Pantomime games like Charades can also help children explore words and concepts, as can drawing games, like Pictionary Jr.

Other Games

You can keep the skills listed in Chapter 2 (see pages 41–43) in mind as you look for other games that may help develop literacy. For example, when we encountered The StoryTelling Game, in which players make up stories incorporating items named and pictured on playing cards, we saw it had the potential to help develop storytelling and story-writing skills as well as vocabulary. (This game is recommended for ages 5 and up but, as with many games, it can be played by younger children with adult assistance.)

Stopping Squabbles Before They Start: "Family Game Night" Troubleshooting

Let's face it, putting assorted family members and possibly pets in one room after a long week and expecting them to get along harmoniously might be a bit unrealistic. In fact, for some families, it's a recipe for disaster. Here are some problems you may encounter and ideas for overcoming them. Maintaining peace is essential. Game night is too valuable to abandon.

* **An older child doesn't enjoy the same games as your younger child.**

   Try having children take turns selecting games to play. If the older child's game choice is too difficult for the younger child, you might consider having the younger one act as the game's emcee, card dealer, score keeper, or the like. This keeps the younger child involved while ensuring the activity is appropriate for her. We have found that many young children love being in charge, and that this often invites opportunities to interact with print. For example, Nell's daughter liked to be the "judge" in the Apples to Apples and Apples to Apples Jr. games (which we highly recommend!). She was able to read some of the cards herself and get help with others.

* **Game night gets too competitive.**

   Some families, and some children, are more competitive than others. If game night is getting too competitive, or a child is having too much difficulty with losing, try a cooperative game. Cooperative games do not render players winners or losers, but rather players work together for a common goal. For example, in Max: A Co-operative Game,

players work together to try to defeat the cat. Try doing an Internet search for "non-competitive games"; you'll find many resources for locating such games to purchase. You can also make cooperative games out of games you already have. For example, instead of playing memory against one another, you might work together to see how many moves it takes the family to make all the matches. Of course, keep written records of your achievements so you can try to beat them next time, and thus bring in literacy in yet another way.

This preschooler is enjoying **Wiggle & Giggle.**

* **Children have ants in their pants.**

Some children have difficulty with the sit time involved in game night, at least when the games take place in the living room. If weather and daylight permit, try some physically active games outdoors. If this isn't possible, consider games that include movement, such as Wiggle & Giggle: The Ball Balancing Physical Game of Fun! And remember that you can make a game out of lots of physical activities. For example, the family might use a stop watch to set a "family record" for the longest duration that any family member can remain standing on one foot, or the family might work together to form as many letters as they can using only their bodies.

* **You've hit a game rut.**

Growing tired of the family's collection of games but don't want or have money to purchase more? Try a game trade with another family—they lend you two favorite games for a month, and you do the same. Or, if you're feeling really ambitious, make up your own game. Some publishers provide kits to make this easier. And, of course, whatever your game, make sure literacy is involved!

Playing With Words: Sounds Like Fun! Phonological Awareness Games

Most children love to play with the sounds in words. This is great news because doing so helps them develop an important set of literacy skills collectively known as *phonological awareness*.[60] Phonological awareness is the awareness of individual sounds and groups of sounds in words, and includes all of the abilities listed in the table below. For example, a child who recognizes that *cheese* has three sounds (/ch/, /e/, and /z/) and *slip* has four (/s/, /l/, /i/, and /p/) demonstrates one kind of phonological awareness. There are several kinds of phonological awareness, as shown in the table:

The ability to:	For example, the child:
Separate words into syllables or beats	Is aware that *apple* has two syllables, and *banana* has three
Recognize rhyming words	Recognizes that *tough* and *stuff* rhyme, and *sing* and *wing* rhyme
Generate rhyming words	Comes up with words that rhyme with *cat: mat, hat, bat,* etc. (this can include nonsense words)
Recognize words that start or end with the same sound	Recognizes that *goat* and *giggle* start with the same sound, and that *ten* and *moon* end with the same sound
Generate words that start or end with the same sound	Can generate several words that begin with the sound at the beginning of *love* or end with the sound at the end of *car*
Blend sounds into words*	Can blend the sounds /n/ /a/ /p/ together to make the word *nap*
Segment words into sounds*	Can break the word *ship* down into its three sounds: /sh/, /i/, /p/
Move sounds around to create new words	Can say *bag* with a /d/ for the /g/ sound to make *bad*

*These two skills seem to be especially important for later literacy development.

It's important to note that phonological awareness doesn't deal with written language or the alphabet—it's simply about children's ability (or lack of ability) to generate and recognize *sounds* through speaking and listening. The box entitled Why Are Phonological Awareness Skills So Important? (page 107) explains how each of the abilities listed above helps prepare children for formal reading and writing instruction. The following pages include some ideas for games to help your child play with the sounds in words.

GAMES

Count the Beats!

In this game, which is appropriate for some older toddlers and preschoolers, children sort things based on the number of beats or syllables in the object's name. For example, children might put *glue, paint,* and *tape* in one pile or group (all one-syllable words); *pencils, paper,* and *scissors* in another pile (all two-syllable words); and a *sharpener* in a pile all by itself (a three-syllable word). Children may enjoy seeing how quickly or accurately they can do this sorting. And you can be on the lookout for items with four syllables or more for children to include. Of course, acting impressed at your child's syllable acumen will encourage him and keep him motivated!

Sometimes it helps if children engage in movement when they break words into syllables, such as patting their legs or clapping, because this makes the task more concrete. We have also found that it helps if you model segmenting words for the child while saying them, as in "pa-per," "pen-cil," and so forth.

Ellen Daugherty Durr

Test Yourself

How many phonemes, or meaningful units of sound, are there in the following words?

a. run   **c.** sheep   **e.** phone

b. bee   **d.** tooth   **f.** rainbow

Answers: a. 3, b. 2, c. 3, d. 3, e. 3, f. 5

Which of the words above has more than one syllable?

Answer: f.

Going on Vacation

In this game, which is usually appropriate for older pre-schoolers, family members take turns announcing things they will take on vacation that begin with the same sound. For example, you might start with "I'm going on vacation and I'm going to take a ball." The next person then needs to think of something else to take on vacation that starts with /b/, such as a *bear* or *barrette*. One by one, each person repeats "I'm going on vacation and I'm going to take a ____" and announces an item until everyone has had a turn or a couple rounds of turns, depending on the number of people. From there, move to another sound and repeat the process. Some families like to have each person repeat all the other items that have been announced before announcing their new item, but we believe this is too difficult for most preschoolers.

You can create variations on this game depending on what your child is working on. For example, if your child is working on separating

Why Are Phonological Awareness Skills So Important?[61]

The ability to . . .	Will eventually help children to . . .
Separate words into syllables or beats	Break down a word into parts to spell or decode/read it—for example, to spell the word *chapter*, break it into *chap* and *ter*
Recognize and generate words that rhyme	Use known words to read new words—for example, to use *catch* to help them read *batch*
Recognize and generate words that start or end with the same sound	Learn to associate particular sounds with particular letters—for example, knowing that *Peter* starts with *p* may help Peter recognize that *purple* also starts with *p*
Blend sounds into words*	"Sound out" words—for example, after saying a sound for each letter in the word *nap* (/n/ /a/ /p/), putting those sounds together to say *nap*
Segment words into sounds*	Spell words—for example, to hear the four sounds in the word *clap* (/c/ /l/ /a/ /p/), so they can spell it
Move sounds around to create new words	Use known words to figure out new words—for example, to use *corn* to help them decode the word *pork*

*These two skills seem to be especially important for later literacy development.

What to Expect: The Typical Order of Phonological Awareness Skills

No two children develop in exactly the same way. That said, there are some rules of thumb—with exceptions, of course—about the order in which children develop phonological awareness skills.[62] Knowing this may help you provide activities that are well matched to your child's current and next steps in development.

1. Skills involving syllables or beats are usually acquired before those involving rhyming, which are in turn acquired before those involving individual phonemes or sounds.

2. Recognition skills often come before generation skills. For example, children are likely to recognize words that rhyme before they can generate words that rhyme.

3. Skills involving the beginnings of words are generally acquired before those involving the ends of words. Skills needed to identify sounds in the middle of words are the last to develop.

4. The ability to blend generally comes before the ability to segment.

5. The ability to move sounds around to create new words is often one of the last skills acquired.

As you foster your child's phonological awareness, use these guidelines to help you choose games that will challenge but not overwhelm him. In other words, choose games that are fun and will make your child feel successful. Of course, simply watching your child carefully will also give you great information that you can use when selecting games and other activities.

words into syllables or beats, you can change the game so that everyone going on vacation has to take something with the same number of beats as the first item given. Or if you are working on generating rhyming words, the rule can be that everyone has to bring something that rhymes with the first word given.

Who Gets Up?

This is a popular game in some child care and preschool settings, but it also works at home. One member of the family—it's best if it's an adult to start—is the caller, who calls upon somebody to stand up. The caller might say, "Anyone whose name starts with /j/ can get up." Or, "Everyone whose name rhymes with *still* can stand up." If standing up isn't an appealing enough incentive, try giving crackers, points, invitations to sit in the favorite chair, or whatever else you feel might work. Remember, to build phonological awareness, the focus should be on sounds—not letters—so you would say the sound /j/ not the letter *j*. Of course, you can create your own variation on the game that involves letter naming to build alphabet skills.

Guess What I'm Saying

In this game, you say a word broken into parts, and your child tries to guess the word. For example, you might say /f/ /un/ for *fun* or /g/ /i/ /g/ /l/ for *giggle*. When you say the sounds—and this goes not just for this game, but any time you are saying individual sounds for children—try to make them sound as natural as possible. For example, say just "ffff" not "ffuh." You won't be able to do this all the time because some sounds are hard to pronounce in isolation, so just do it to the degree you can. Otherwise your child may come up with something like *fuhruhoguh* when you intend *frog*.

Collaborative Productions

To develop children's segmenting skills, play a variation on Guess What I'm Saying, in which the child segments the words into sounds and you have to guess the words by blending the sounds together. Be aware that this variation may be difficult for your child, at least until she has a handle on the original blending version. (See What to Expect: The Typical Order of Phonological Awareness Skills, page 108.)

We have found that Guess What I'm Saying is most fun for children when you play up how impressed you are when they correctly guess the word, and say things like, "I think I'm going to trick you on this next one . . ." (when you're pretty sure you won't). Of course, this depends on your individual style with your child. We also find children like it when you pick words they find funny. Have fun with it!

Giving Performances

The living room is also a perfect site for performance activities that build literacy, including singing, storytelling, and puppetry.

Singing

For many families, gathering around the piano to sing songs together in four-part harmony is something you watch in old movies, not something you actually do. It is as far from the reality of 21st-century households as butter churns. But singing is a wonderful activity that is not only fun, but can help build your child's phonological awareness, vocabulary, musical skills, such as pitch and rhythm, and general cultural literacy.

Using Singing for Recognizing and Generating Rhyming Words

So many songs for young children contain rhyming words. Here's a familiar example, "Twinkle, Twinkle, Little Star":

> Twinkle, twinkle, little star
>
> How I wonder what you are.
>
> Up above the world so high
>
> Like a diamond in the sky.
>
> Twinkle, twinkle, little star
>
> How I wonder what you are.

A more modern song is "Five Green and Speckled Frogs":

Many popular songs come in picture-book versions. Your librarian or bookseller can help you look for board versions of a specific song, or you can browse the variety of song-based books they have.

> Five green and speckled frogs,
>
> sat on a speckled log,
>
> eating some most delicious bugs.
>
> Yum. Yum.
>
> One jumped into the pool,
>
> where it was nice and cool.
>
> Now there are four green, speckled frogs,
>
> Glub. Glub.
>
> [and so on until there are none]

Singing these songs to infants sets the stage for building phonological awareness. But if your child is a toddler or young preschooler, you should help him learn to sing the songs himself. With older preschoolers, focus on the rhyming words, which you might explain as "words that have ending parts that sound the same." You can identify the rhyming words for your child or see if he can pick out the words himself.

Some songs provide opportunities for children to generate rhyming words—for example, "Down by the Bay":

> Down by the bay,
>
> Where the watermelons grow,
>
> Back to my home
>
> I dare not go.
>
> For if I do
>
> My mother will say,
>
> "Did you ever see a _____
>
> wearing a _____
>
> Down by the bay?"

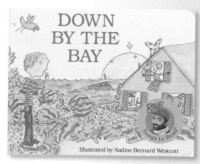

Children's singer Raffi has a series, Songs to Read, many of which are available in both board book and paper form.

Have your child help you fill in the blanks with rhyming words, such as *cat/hat* or *some ants/some pants*, and so on. Alternative versions include:

> Did you ever see a _____ eating
>
> a _____
>
> Did you ever see a _____ walk
>
> with a _____

"Did you ever see a _____ walk with a _____" may be a good one to start with because its potential to generate sensible word pairs is greater than the other two fill-in passages—for example, *dog/ frog, duck/truck,* and *ape/grape.* The possibilities are virtually endless!

And what should you do if your child uses non-sense words—for example, "Have you ever seen a *horse* eating a *lorse*"? We believe it is fine. In addition to being hysterically funny to many children, it suggests

Song Secrets

Did you know that many songs for young children are sung to the same tune, such as "The Alphabet Song" and "Twinkle, Twinkle, Little Star"? This may be a big help for you and your child because it means often you don't have to learn new tunes in order to learn new songs.

they are truly able to generate rhyming words rather than just memorize word pairs they've heard you use. You might point out, though, that these are "silly words" that don't mean anything so that your child does not become confused.

Using Singing for Moving Sounds Around to Create New Words

Moving sounds around is a difficult skill for most young children. So it's comforting to know that there are many songs that can provide fun practice.

One well-known song, "The Name Game," helps you address that and other phonological awareness skills.

Shir-ley Shir-ley bo Bir-ley Bo-na-na Fan-na fo Fir-ley Mee my mo Mir-ley Shir-ley!

Singing this song takes practice, but we have seen even young 3-year-olds do it. Children younger than that may enjoy hearing you sing it.

"Apples and Bananas" is another song that requires moving sounds around, and it may be a little less challenging than "The Name Game" because the same ten sounds are always used. They are the long vowel sounds (/ā/ as in *ape*, /ē/ as in *eagle*, /ī/ as in *ice*, /ō/ as in *open*, /ū/ as in *unicorn*) and the short vowel sounds (/ă/ as in *apple*, /ĕ/ as in *egg*, /ĭ/ as in *igloo*, /ŏ/ as in *octopus*, /ŭ/ as in *upside down*):

> I like to ēat, ēat, ēat, apples and bananas (repeat)
>
> I like to āet, āet, āet, āpples and banānās (repeat)
>
> I like to ēat, ēat, ēat, ēeples and banēenēes (repeat)
>
> I like to īet, īet, īet, īepples and banīenīes (repeat)
>
> [and so on for the rest of long vowel and short vowel sounds]

I like to eat eat eat ap-ples and ba-na-nas I like to eat eat eat ap-ples and ba-na-nas.

"Old MacDonald" can be adapted similarly. As with "Apples and Bananas," this version of "Old McDonald" can encourage your child to move sounds around to create new words as well as help develop other phonological awareness skills, such as generating words that start with the same sound. Instead of just singing:

> Old MacDonald had a farm
>
> E – I – E – I – O . . .

sing:

> Old MacDonald had a farm
>
> LE – LI – LE – LI – LO
>
> And on this farm he had an /l/ [the sound, not the letter]
>
> LE – LI – LE – LI – LO
>
> With an /l/ /l/ here and an /l/ /l/ there
>
> Here an /l/, there an /l/, everywhere an /l/, /l/
>
> Old MacDonald had an /l/
>
> LE – LI – LE – LI – LO
>
> [and so on for different sounds]

A favorite song in many childcare settings and preschool classes that requires moving sounds around and other phonological awareness skills is "Willoughby Wallaby Woo":

> Willoughby wallaby woo
>
> An elephant sat on you
>
> Willoughby wallaby wee
>
> An elephant sat on me
>
> Willoughby wallaby Wommy
>
> An elephant sat on Mommy
>
> Willoughby wallaby Waddy
>
> An elephant sat on Daddy
>
> [and so on for different names of family and friends]

You might have your own ideas about songs that can build phonological awareness. We encourage you to work them into the family repertoire as well—you'll be building important literacy skills, and togetherness, in the process.

Tongue Twisters: Terrific Teaching Tools for Tots

Tongue twisters are great for helping children recognize and generate words that start with the same sound. There are many tongue twisters, some you may already know (such as *Peter Piper Picked a Peck of Pickled Peppers* and *She Sells Sea Shells by the Sea Shore*, which uses two sounds, /sh/ and /s/) and some that may be new, like the one below.

Shelly shouldn't shake saltshakers, should she?

If your child enjoys tongue twisters, you might look for a book of them, such as *Six Sick Sheep: 101 Tongue Twisters* by Joanna Cole and Stephanie Calmenson.

Do not assume that your child will realize that the words within a tongue twister begin with the same sound. Explicitly point out this fact, perhaps identifying the letter or letters associated with that sound.

You may also want to try your hand at writing new tongue twisters with your child; this will give her a chance to practice generating words with the same beginning sound. You might use your child's or a friend's name and an apt adjective to help get her started. (Notice the opportunity for vocabulary development, too.) For example:

Magical Mario . . .

Princely Paul . . .

Silly Steven . . .

Elegant Emily . . .

Repeating the target sound multiple times and/or giving your child an engaging, inspirational category may help her come up with words to complete the tongue twister. For example, after giving her the starter "Magical Mario . . . ," you might repeat the /m/ sound and give the category foods. Your child might then say, "macaroni," "meatballs," and "milk." From there, work with her to assemble the words into a tongue twister:

Magical Mario must make macaroni, meatballs, and milk!

You might even work with your child to illustrate her tongue twisters using children's drawings, magazine pictures, and/or photographs. Then make sure your child gets a chance to share her creation with other family members and friends.

Avery ate acorns and ably aided apes.

Eleven Enriching Books for Building Phonological Awareness

Looking for more ways to build phonological awareness? Try reading aloud any of these books, which emphasize specific phonological awareness skills.

Separating words into syllables or beats:

Nearly any book works well for this, especially those with a strong rhythm, for example:

Silly Sally
by A. Wood

We're Going on a Bear Hunt
by M. Rosen

Recognizing and/or generating rhyming words:

There are so many books to develop this skill! We made ourselves stop at five.

Duck in the Truck
by J. Alborough

Hop on Pop
by Dr. Seuss

Is Your Mama a Llama?
by D. Guarino

Room on the Broom
by J. Donaldson

The Seals on the Bus
by L. Hort

Recognizing words that start with the same sound:

Again, many books work well for building this skill, including the alphabet books listed in Chapter 6. Also consider:

Sheep in a Shop
by N. Shaw

Moving sounds around to create new words:

There aren't as many books that support this skill, but here are a few.

Ook the Book and Other Silly Rhymes
by L. Rovetch

Runny Babbit: A Billy Sook
by S. Silverstein

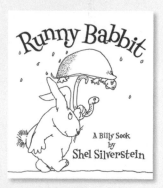

There's a Wocket in My Pocket
by Dr. Seuss

Storytelling

Many families have a sweet aunt who tells wonderful stories at holiday dinners. But did you know she is doing a lot more than keeping family lore alive? She's helping to build children's literacy. Research suggests that children who are exposed to stories have stronger language and literacy development.[63] So tell stories—about things that have happened to you, things that have happened to your child, and so on. We find that our children especially love stories involving funny things they have said or done, about things they have done with us, or about embarrassing things that have happened to us.

You will probably find that your child develops an affection for particular stories and, therefore, wants to hear them again and again. Hearing stories retold many times can deepen the child's understanding of the structure, language, and content of the story. Over time, even a very young child can help you tell the tale. A favorite story in Nell's family derives from a trip to a local discount store. As Nell and her then 2-year-old daughter Julia were shopping, Julia found a bath bead that had apparently fallen out of a package and onto the floor. Nell noticed Julia holding the small object and asked what she had in her hand. Julia

Ellen Daugherty Durr

replied, "A choking hazard: I'm gonna go choke on it!" and ran away. Over time, as Nell has told the story, she has given Julia more and more of a role—from initially just repeating what Nell said, to later giving details such as the name of the store where they were shopping, to finally telling the whole story on her own. By doing this, Nell gives Julia the opportunity to develop storytelling skills and to see how stories can entertain.

Like Julia, many children enjoy stories in which they are the central character. These can be true stories, such as the story of when they were born or joined the family, or make-believe stories in which they take on fantastic roles as pirates, princesses, or porcupines. Susan's daughter Violet alternated between wanting to hear about how she came to be adopted from China and how she would be a basketball-playing princess that discovers a new planet one day. The beauty of storytelling is there are only the rules you decide to enforce.

You can also encourage your child to tell you a story largely of his own. Sometimes simply asking, "Can you tell me a story?" will set the wheels in motion. If you are asking for a fictional story, use a familiar prompt like "Once upon a time there was . . . " If you are asking for a true story, use something like "Do you remember what happened on the boat?" Some children benefit from a series of questions to help them develop their story, which you can ask as they're telling it, at appropriate points. Those questions might include:

Who is in your story?

Where did this happen?

What happened first?

And then what happened?

What happened in the end?

If your child is comfortable with storytelling, give him an audience—someone who hasn't heard his story before. This will provide him with practice in telling stories that contain all the necessary elements to make sense for an audience. You could also write the stories down, but in that case be sure your child understands the story is to be written, rather than told, as he may wish to use more book-like language for a written story. (See page 96 for more about taking dictation from children.)

Puppetry

Children can use puppets not only to entertain adults and other children but also to promote their blossoming literacy. Puppet play builds writing (that is, composing) skills as children act out stories. It can also build listening and reading comprehension skills when children develop stories for performances or adapt stories from books. Puppet play also allows children to try out newly acquired vocabulary and explore themes such as "right and wrong" or "good and evil."

Puppets can be original characters that spring from your child's imagination or they can be inspired by characters from books. They can be bought at the store or made by hand. Here are four easy ways to create puppets:

* **Stick Puppets** Have your child make character shapes out of thick paper and attach them to popsicle sticks, tongue depressors, paint stirrers, or rulers.

* **Finger Puppets** Give your child gloves and have her decorate each finger to depict a different character.

* **Spoon Puppets** Invite your child to paint faces onto wooden spoons of various sizes, attach yarn for hair, and even use fabric to create clothing.

* **Paper-Bag Puppets** Have your child use markers, yarn, and other materials to turn a simple paper bag into a wonderful puppet.

David Ammer

Raymond Coutu

A couch makes a perfectly fine stage.

You can buy commercial puppet theaters; many doorway and table-top models are available, but they are typically over $50. If you don't want to invest in a commercial theater, you can create your own with a tension rod across a doorway and an old sheet, or a table and tablecloth. The back of the couch also works well.

Children can participate in puppet play in a variety of ways, depending on their developmental level and interests. Infants may enjoy watching the show and exploring the puppets. Toddlers may begin to take part in creating the show, perhaps playing a small but important role. Preschoolers may want to orchestrate much of the show themselves. Some children may enjoy selling tickets to the show in advance or creating a program for the show. Nell's daughter even created signs requesting that no cell phones or iPods be used during the performance!

If puppets don't strike your child's fancy, he may enjoy acting out stories with dolls, action figures, or stuffed animals, or he may have fun becoming the characters himself. All of these activities yield the benefits described at the start of this section—fostering writing, listening, and reading comprehension. So play away!

PERFORMANCES

Watching Television and Video

Do you prohibit television or video watching for fear it will harm your child's development? Or do you allow television or video watching but feel guilty? Or perhaps you haven't thought about it one way or the other. Television and video players are part of the living rooms of almost every U.S. and Canadian household. In this section we'll explain how you can use them to support literacy development, and we'll outline some viewing practices to avoid.

Whether TV and video are "good" or "bad" depends on the program, and the conditions under which your child watches it. Here are some benefits of TV and video viewing:

* Some programs have been shown to improve specific literacy skills in children, such as letter knowledge and vocabulary. These include the extensively researched Public Broadcasting Service (PBS) programs *Sesame Street* (ages 2 to 5) and *Between the Lions* (ages 4 to 7). Other PBS programs have been studied to a lesser degree but results are promising, including *Arthur* (ages 4 to 8), *Barney* (ages 2 to 5), *Martha Speaks* (ages 4 to 7), *Reading Rainbow* (ages 4 to 8), *Super WHY!* (ages 3 to 6), and *Word World* (ages 3 to 5).

* Other programs have the potential to build vocabulary or knowledge of story structure, such as video read-alouds of storybooks, high-quality children's movies, or *Faery Tale Theatre*, which is no longer on TV but is available on DVD.

* And many programs have the potential to build knowledge about the world—from wildlife documentaries to adventure programs to history specials and more. Some programs are designed especially to build world knowledge in young children, such as *Peep and the Big Wide World*. At Susan's house, Discovery Channel's *Shark Week* is untouchable and has been since her 23-year-old was 2. Watching those programs prompted his interest in reading shark books, writing books about sharks, and even dictating a letter to the vice president about the need to protect sharks in American waters.

Television and Video for Children 0 to 2?

You may notice that all of the ages we have been referring to in this section are age 2 or above. There is little research on television and video for children younger than 2, and the studies that do exist have found mixed results. Infants might learn to recognize a new word or object, and they can have an emotional response to what's on screen. But very young children learn much more—and better—from real life people and experiences.[64] At least one organization—the American Academy of Pediatrics—has called for no television in the first two years of life. We would not go that far (well, Susan would) but instead would suggest that you take even greater care in selecting viewing opportunities for your infant and young toddler. You should keep in mind all the factors we discussed on page 120; keep viewing time to a minimum; and remain present and engaged during nearly all of your infant's and your toddler's viewing.

All of this said, there are some videos designed for very young children that we like a lot. *Baby Mugs*, for example, shows a series of photographs and video clips of baby faces set to music. Nell's daughter loved this, and it is difficult to see what harm there could be in her watching that, in addition to looking at her many baby face books and interacting with real babies. Notably, Nell's son showed very little interest in the *Baby Mugs* video and so she did not watch it with him. Annie and her son enjoyed watching *Eebee's Adventures* DVDs together. Eebee (a puppet) interacts with real babies, young children, and adults around real-life objects and play scenarios, such as building ramps and rolling balls, stacking cups or blocks, and playing with laundry. After watching an episode, Annie would bring out similar objects for the two of them to play with together. As we know, every child is different, and we need to monitor each individual child's response.

Some books appropriate for infants and toddlers have been set to video, such as *Goodnight Moon* by Margaret Wise Brown, with video by HBO Kids Video.

Don't Let the Television Take Over

In Chapter 3 we noted that many people tend to read things because they are there. People also tend to watch things that are there. To avoid having television and video viewing become a default activity, and to keep better and more deliberate control over what your child does and does not watch, consider these tips:

* **Keep a television only in rooms where you are in control.** The child's bedroom and the playroom are, in most cases, not a good place for a television. Television in a child's bedroom has been linked to more time watching, greater risk for obesity, and sleep problems.[65] You are less likely to be able to co-view or control viewing, and isolation, with each member of the family in his own electronic kingdom, is a likely result.

* **Keep the television behind closed doors.** We find that just the extra step of having to open a couple of cabinet doors to watch the television makes it more likely it will be on just when you want it to be.

* **Do not leave the television on.** As a general rule, the television should be turned on when the family wants to watch a specific program or video and turned off when that viewing is finished. One recent study found that children under 2 years are exposed to about 4 hours of background television per day.[66] Television that is on in the background has been shown to interrupt and shorten a child's play and it can distract adults who are playing with their children.[67] Television in these instances is harming, rather than helping learning.

* **Plan television viewing.** When practical, plan in advance what you and the family will watch (and therefore will not watch) during the day or over a week.

* **Offer alternative activities.** If your child expresses interest in watching TV at a time when you do not want him to, or in watching a program you do not want him to, rather than just not allowing it, offer a fun activity in its place.

* **Encourage interest.** On the flip side, when there *is* a program you would like your child to watch, work to encourage interest in that program by telling the child what it is about, why you think he might like it, why other children like it, and so on. And when the program starts, be sure you are with your child to help explain and set the context for it.

David Armistead

Sometimes silly videos inspire silly interactive play. In this case, Sesame Street's *Sing Yourself Silly* did the trick.

Beyond these, however, there are many programs that are probably not helpful, and potentially harmful, to literacy development. Annie and Nell did a study of the top ten programs most watched by children ages 2 to 5,[68] most of which air on commercial television. In general, these programs contained very few examples of reading or writing. To watch these programs, you would think the world was devoid of, rather than bursting with, print. Moreover, several programs sometimes sent negative messages about literacy to children. In *The Fairly Odd Parents*, for example, the main character abuses books in a variety of ways, from shooting slingshots at books flying through the air to using books as water skis to having another person catch a book in his mouth and bury it in the ground.

Another thing to keep in mind is that programs on commercial television usually feature advertisements. In fact, an hour of television may contain 10-12 minutes of advertising.[69] This sets the bar higher: Not only does the program need to be worth the 48-50 minutes spent watching it, it needs to be worth the additional minutes the child will spend watching ads during it!

What's a Parent to Do?

Research and common sense suggest that what children watch, as well as how they watch, is important. We urge you to consider the following guidelines.

Select Programs Carefully

Ask yourself:

* Does my child enjoy the show?
* Is the show designed exclusively or in part for children around my child's age or developmental level?
* Will the child learn anything positive from the show? (For example, is it *designed* to be educational, or does it have a rich story line or convey interesting, sound information?)
* Will commercials be shown?
* Is there something better available for my child to watch?
* Do I have the time to view and talk about the show with my child?

Think About What Else Your Child Would Be Doing

Consider what children would or could be doing if television and video weren't available. If they would be testing your patience as you tried to fix dinner, TV or video may be a good choice. If they would otherwise be reading or visiting with you, TV or video is not a good choice—*you* are a better one!

Practice Moderation

Figure out how much time you want your child to spend in front of the TV screen and stick to it. Thirty minutes? One hour? Keep in mind that heavy TV viewing (more than three hours per day) is linked to a number of negative outcomes for children, such as less time spent in social interaction and more aggressive behaviors. Also, consider your child's time spent with apps, online games, video games, and other electronic media. These all add up, and there should be moderation across media. An important consideration is whether there is so much screen time that it is displacing other valuable activities, such as reading and writing, playing outdoors, or interacting with you or other children. If so, that's a problem. If it is replacing time spent watching you do laundry or coloring in a coloring book, the time spent in front of the TV screen may be well worth it. See Don't Let the Television Take Over (page 122) for other ways to practice moderation. Moderation also includes your own time in front of big and small screens. A 2013 study found that children from 5 years of age through adolescence picked up on and reflected their parents media habits.[70] The more often you watch, scroll, and type, the more likely (and more often!) your child will, too.

Watch and Talk About Programs With Your Child

When parents and children "co-view" programs, research suggests that children's learning is enhanced. Of course, this enhanced learning only takes place when meaningful conversation accompanies the viewing. For example, merely saying the name of a character on screen probably won't teach your child much. However, using adjectives to describe the character, asking the child what she thinks about what the character did or said, and so on, probably will.[71] Consider talking during TV and video viewing in the way you talk during reading. Ask questions, make comments, and make connections between the program's content and your child's life.

Mute the commercials, if there are any, so you can talk without competing with the ads, or use the pause button to facilitate a discussion.

Ryan J. Verhey-Henke

Follow Up With Reading

Some television programs, such as *Clifford, Martha Speaks*, and *Arthur*, and many children's movies, are based on books. So, after viewing, it makes perfect sense to read the book upon which the program or movie is based. You can also find a book that was showcased during an episode of *Super WHY!* or on the *Reading Rainbow* app that your child particularly liked. But remember to select books carefully— be sure they are of high quality and of interest to your child. Books based on TV programs (as opposed to the other way around) tend to be poorly written and are usually not worth reading unless your child is highly motivated to hear the book.

Develop Media Literacy Skills

When you spend time with your child in front of the TV screen, seize the opportunity to develop media literacy skills— or higher-order thinking skills used to analyze the programming's content. Faith Rogow, founder of the Alliance for a Media Literate America, suggests some of the following strategies for encouraging preschoolers to think about what they see on TV[72]:

Collaborative Productions

Ask, "Who Is the Storyteller?"
Just as there are authors of books and other print material, there are "authors" of movies, television programs, and commercials. You'll get different answers to this question depending on your child's age—which is fine. For example, if your young child is watching *Arthur*, she might say that Arthur is the storyteller. An older child might be able to understand that there are writers, producers, and networks "behind the scenes." Just talking with children about this question is an important first step.

Talk About and Retell Events on Television and in Movies As we have mentioned, it is important to discuss what your child is watching, so ask him questions and listen to what he has to say. Have your child tell others about all (this is difficult for most young children) or parts of what they have watched. Starting to talk about the messages programs and movies send is also important and should benefit your child in the long run.

Evaluate Television and Video From very early on, encourage your child to evaluate the media he or she views. Ask questions like "Did you like that?" "What did you think of that?" "What was your favorite part?" "Was there anything you didn't like?" Model your own evaluations as well. If you see something sexist in a move, for example, tell your child what you saw, that you didn't like it, and why. And if you really like the moral or message of a program or video, or the performance of a particular actor, or the like, make sure you let your child know.

Use Television and Movie Lingo Another suggestion from Faith Rogow is to use the lingo of the media. For example, when Nell's daughter was in preschool, Nell used terms such as "special effects" and "actors/actresses" to help her daughter understand what she was, and was not, seeing. You can also focus on the sounds in programming, and talk about how different sounds and music make your child feel. If the programming includes commercials, use this term, and talk about how these differ from other kinds of programming. Help your child see ways that advertisers try to get you to buy their products.

The ability to understand and evaluate media critically is vital to life in our society. We are bombarded with images, ideas, information, and opinions that can overwhelm and mislead us if we don't use critical thinking. With some effort, you can develop these skills in your child and help her benefit from the wonders of the big and small screen.

Concluding Thoughts

The living room is for living, and literacy is a big part of life. Take advantage of the many opportunities the living room offers for building literacy—by playing games, telling stories, putting on puppet shows, watching television and video wisely, and engaging in many other activities together. In the next chapter, we head to the bedroom to explore the many opportunities for enriching literacy there.

CHAPTER 6

In the Bedroom

*I*n Trevor's bedroom, you will find many typical toddler toys, including stuffed animals, puzzles, and trains. You will also find shelves containing favorite books, such as *The Monster at the End of This Book* (by Jon Stone, illustrated by Mike Smollin) and *One Fish Two Fish Red Fish Blue Fish* (by Dr. Seuss). And you'll find all sorts of things Trevor uses when he plays—

a "doctor's bag"
and stethoscope,
play food, and his
beloved building
blocks.

Ellen Daugherty Durr

If you walk
by his bedroom
at naptime or
bedtime, you will most likely hear Trevor asking

his parents to read *Love You Forever* (by Robert

Munsch and Sheila McGraw), even though he

has heard it so many times he can "read" it

himself. After breakfast or before lunch, you may

hear "Dr. Trevor" diagnosing his patient, a stuffed

animal, with a cold. Or you may hear Trevor

serving pizza and ice cream to customers of his

imaginary restaurant. You may even hear him

constructing a new metropolis with the blocks

on his bedroom floor. All of these activities and others happen every day in Trevor's bedroom.

Trevor is fast becoming a literate person in the comfort of his bedroom. By reading with their parents and engaging in pretend play, Trevor and other young children like him participate in activities that are not only fun for them, but also important for their literacy development. In this chapter, we discuss two activities that promote literacy that are commonly carried out in children's bedrooms: read-alouds and dramatic (or pretend) play. In the first section, we discuss:

* Why reading aloud is important
* What good parent-child read-alouds look and sound like
* How to create comfortable spaces for read-alouds

In the second section, we discuss the connection between dramatic play and literacy, and we suggest ways to encourage your child to incorporate literacy into dramatic play.

Finally, we include ideas about how to stock children's rooms with toys that will boost their development, and ideas for integrating literacy into two favorite bedroom-based activities: building with blocks and putting puzzles together.

Reading Aloud: An Avenue Into Literacy

There's no doubt you have heard the advice "Read with your child every day!" And those who suggest doing so are absolutely right! Reading to children and having them pretend-read to you are essential activities. Some researchers even insist that sharing books is the most significant thing that parents can do to promote literacy.[73] Reading together can also strengthen ties with your child because it gives you a reason to spend quality time together.

So the experts' advice is sensible, but what those experts typically don't tell you is *how* to read with young children, especially before they enter school. In the section that follows, you will learn not only why reading aloud is important, but also how to do it so your child reaps the full benefits.

What Is a Read-Aloud?

When you read to your child, do you sit down with one book and read it straight through? If so, you might be missing aspects of the book that are really interesting and important to your child. You might be missing opportunities to promote literacy, too. Instead of the read-straight-through approach, we advocate interactive read-alouds.[74]

In an interactive read-aloud, you stop, talk, explain, question, comment, and really dig in and engage with the text. You are responsive, just as you are when you're promoting your child's oral language. Here are some guidelines to follow when you read aloud:

* Allow your child to choose the reading material frequently.

* Take your child's lead in determining what to talk about in a book.

* Address questions that your child asks along the way (even if that answer is "I'm not sure, that's a good question. Let's think about how we can find an answer to that.")

* Ask your child questions.

* Make comments about what you notice in the book, connections you are making, your response to the book ("That's funny."), and so on.

* Encourage your child to chime in.

* Offer child-friendly explanations of words in the text that may be unfamiliar to your child.

* Stop if your child becomes bored or needs to move on to a different activity.

David Ammer

In addition, reading with expression is important when reading aloud to your child. Using different voices for different characters, showing emotions on your face, and even acting out different parts can make the text come alive.

Common Questions About Reading Aloud

Inevitably, everyday life brings different challenges to reading aloud—for example, your child might not want to sit long enough for you to get through a whole book, or your child doesn't seem to enjoy the read-aloud experience. Never force your child to listen to or engage in a read-aloud. If you find yourself spending more time getting your child to sit still and pay attention than reading and talking about the book, it's a sign to stop. Reading aloud and engaging with books should be enjoyable experiences. Children should not associate negative feelings with them. With that in mind, here are some questions that might have crossed your mind:

What If My Child Is Always on the Move?

Children have a lot of energy. For many of them, it's hard to listen to and talk about books for long stretches of time. Here are some strategies that can make reading aloud a joy for you and your active child:

* Consider reading in short chunks.

* Remember that your child can still be listening to what you're reading while also doing something else.

* Wait to read until your child is in a better state for it—this may mean a change of location, such as reading aloud during car rides (by someone not driving, of course) or reading during bath time.

* Find books that involve movement so that your child can be both physical and involved in the read-aloud at the same time. There are many great choices out there, including *Eyes, Nose, Fingers, and Toes* by Judy Hindley, *From Head to Toe* by Eric Carle, and *Head, Shoulders, Knees, and Toes: And Other Action Rhymes* illustrated by Zita Newcome, which includes many familiar rhymes such as "Pat-a-cake" and "Itsy, Bitsy Spider," as well as some that may be new to you, such as "Five Little Firefighters." A number of the rhymes include illustrations showing movements to go along with the rhymes. You might also look at books that include sign language along with print as a way to engage your child with read-alouds, such as books published by Garlic Press.

Your child will likely enjoy the physical activity involved when you read *Knees and Toes*.

What If My Child Doesn't Seem to Enjoy Being Read To?

We begin the answer to this question with more questions: The last time you read to your child, was there sufficient space for both of you to sit comfortably? Could your child see the pages clearly? Did she have an opportunity to point to the pictures, ask questions, make comments, or talk about her thoughts about what was being read? Did the topic or genre of the book appeal to her? Was something else going on that might have been distracting her? Was it the best time of day for you or your child to engage in a read-aloud?

Answering these questions may help you uncover reasons why your child doesn't seem to like being read to. Homing in on what you think might be problematic will help you figure out how to resolve it so that your child comes to like, and perhaps even love, read-alouds.

Do Read-Alouds Have to Take Place at Bedtime?

Bedtime seems like the quintessential time for reading aloud. But it may not always be the best choice. There are a number of reasons why. Some children become so preoccupied with other parts of the bedtime routine, or with bedtime conflicts, that they are not able to concentrate on the read-aloud. Other times, children are too exhausted and/or wired at bedtime. Some children even fall asleep during read-aloud, which is okay, but it means you should read aloud at other times, too. After all, we don't want children to associate reading with sleep! If any of these circumstances sounds familiar, then finding another time for read-alouds may be the best solution. Who said that bedtime stories must be reserved for bedtime only? Waking up with a book is a great way to ease into the day.

It may also be the case that, after a long day, some parents aren't at their best to read with patience and passion. If you know this about yourself, again, look for other times to read aloud. Take our advice: Where and when you read with your child is less important than what and how you read with him.

Am I the Only One Who Should Read Aloud With My Child?

Most children love to have a parent read to them. But it can be a treat to have others read to them, such as an older sibling, a grandparent or other relative, a babysitter, or a neighbor. Another "reader" you might consider is videotapes, DVDs, and audiotapes. See Chapter 5 for more about this.

Why Are Read-Alouds Important?

Like Trevor, most young children love being read to by a grown-up. Reading can transform a bedroom into a new, literacy-rich world, and it can help transform children into readers and writers! How? By enhancing many aspects of literacy development, including these five we introduced in Chapter 2:

* concepts of print
* letter-sound knowledge
* vocabulary
* world knowledge
* comprehension

Most teachers understand these critical aspects of literacy and help students become skilled in them every day. But parents may not be all that familiar with them or their importance. So in this section we address them individually.

One reminder, though: The bedroom, as any room, can make a difference in children's literacy experiences. With the busy lives we lead, we need to provide a literacy "safe haven," in which we are fostering our children's enjoyment of read-alouds. (See Chapter 3 for ways to organize and enhance the physical environment to support your efforts.)

Concepts of Print

How do you hold a book? Where do you begin to read on a page? In what direction do you read the print? Often, we do not stop to think about how print works and how we deal with it—these things are second nature. But the idea of "concepts of print" requires that we make these matters apparent for young children. The concepts of print involve basic understandings about how print and books "work": realizing, for example, that books have a front and a back, are read from left to right, have pictures that give us information about the text, have spaces separating words (concept of word), and have words that don't change between readings. Children must learn these concepts to become good readers, and one important way that can happen is through read-alouds.[75]

Here are some ideas for enhancing your child's concepts of print.

Hold, Open, and Read the Book in Front of Your Child By doing this, you demonstrate how to handle and use a book appropriately. In time, even very young children begin to take over the responsibilities of holding the book or turning the pages.

Raymond Coutu

These two young boys are coming to understand concepts of print as they explore a book on firefighters together.

Alison Billman

Read-alouds provide many opportunities to model for your child how we hold a book, open a book, and read the text in books.

Track the Words as You Read Run your finger under the words as you read to help your child see that we read words (not pictures), that we read from left to right and top to bottom, and that words are separated by spaces. Tracking is also useful for introducing punctuation marks and, eventually, to help with word identification.

Draw Attention to Book Parts By discussing terms such as *front*, *back*, *beginning*, *middle*, and *end*, you help your child learn about the parts of books and where to find them.

Children, too, can start to track print themselves as they read or look at a book. Again, this reminds them that it is the print we read, not the pictures.

Show How to Find Certain Sections of the Book Many informative/explanatory books include access features such as a table of contents, an index, headings, and captions—features that your child will need to know how to use. You can help by showing him how to use these features to find information. For instance, your child may become interested in finding out about tadpoles. You can show him how to use the index of an informational text to read more about these creatures. Remember, a book isn't the only tool for talking about and modeling how to explore text. Other reading materials, such as children's magazines, poems, nursery rhymes, and even recipes, can also be used. (See Chapter 3 for a list of many different kinds of reading material available for children.)

Letter-Sound Knowledge

Have you ever heard the comment that English is a difficult language to learn and use? One reason why some people feel this is because of the relationship between letters and sounds in English: There are 44 different meaningful sounds in the English language, and only 26 letters.[76] (See Some Things You Should Know About Sounds and Letters in English, page 138.) As readers and writers, we need to know the sound or sounds that go with a particular letter, not just the letter name itself. And the letter name does not always indicate what the sound is. A letter may have multiple sounds associated with it, such as the letter *c*. (Think of *cereal* versus *car* versus *cheese*, and so on.) The name of a letter may not actually begin with the letter's sound (the name of the letter *m* begins with the /ĕ/ sound, as in "em") and a letter name may not even include a sound represented by the letter (such as the name of the letter *w*). Although learning letter names is important, learning sounds associated with letters is even more important—this is the information we actually use when reading and writing.

Kristin Moses

Letter Names That May Confuse Your Child:

The names of the letters *h, w,* and *y* may be particularly confusing to your child because the common sound(s) of the letter aren't even in the letter's name! You might find your child writing "wg" for "dog" because the name for *w* actually starts with the /d/ sound. With these and all letters, it is important to teach the sounds as well as the names of the letters.[77]

A reminder: Throughout this book, when we talk about sounds, we use two slash marks. So the sound commonly represented by the letter *d* would be denoted like this: /d/.

Some Things You Should Know About Sounds and Letters in English

As we mentioned, the connection between letters and sounds in the English language is not always straightforward. The table below includes some issues that might come up when dealing with letter-sound correspondence, as well as some examples and some suggestions for what you might say to your child about inconsistencies—in general, clarity and honesty are the best policies when confronting the fact that letters and sounds don't always match up the way one would think.

The issue:	Some examples:	What to say about it:
Several letters stand for at least two different sounds.	The letter *c* stands for the sound at the beginning of *cereal* and *car*. *g*: soft in *giraffe*, hard in *grapes* *a*: short in *apple*, long in *ape* *u*: short in *umbrella*, long in *unicorn* This issue also applies to the letters *e*, *i*, *o*, and others.	If looking at an alphabet book with hard and soft *c* words, say, "Remember, *c* sometimes stands for the /s/ sound and sometimes stands for the /k/ sound." If your child guesses that the word *giraffe* begins with *j*, say, "Yes, *j* is one letter that stands for the /j/ sound. What's another letter that stands for that sound?"
Some letters stand for a different sound when paired with another letter.	When the letter *s* is followed by the letter *h*, it usually sounds like /sh/, as in *shell*, not /s/ as in *sand*. When the letter *t* is followed by the letter *h*, it usually sounds like /th/ as in *the*, not /t/ as in *top*. This also happens with *c* (/ch/), *p* (/ph/), *o* (/ow/), and others.	When your child seems confused about seeing *shells* begin with an *s*, you might say, "Yes, that is strange. We actually spell the /sh/ sound with two letters together, *s* and *h*."
Vowels often sound different when followed by /m/, /n/, or /r/.	When a vowel sound is followed by *m* or *n*, it sounds different, such as the first sound in *ant* as opposed to *apple*. When a vowel sound is followed by an *r*, it sounds different, too, such as the first sound in *art* or *orange*.	When your child can't hear that *art* starts with *a*, try addressing this by saying, "You can't hear /a/ in *art*, but it starts with an *a*. Sometimes we spell the /ar/ sound *ar*."

What not to do: Don't distort words to try to make them sound like their spellings. This may confuse your child, mislead her, and undermine her ability to hear or pronounce.

There are a number of ways to point out letter-sound connections, especially during read-alouds.
Reading aloud alphabet books, in particular, can offer
many opportunities to showcase letter-sound connections. (See Fifteen Fabulous Alphabet Books on pages
141–142). For instance, check out *A Is for Artist: A Getty
Museum Alphabet* by the J. Paul Getty Museum. This
book contains beautiful illustrations—real, classic paint-
ings hanging in the Getty Museum—for each letter.
There are also useful vocabulary words included ("G is

for grape" and "U is for umbrella") and more unique ones, too ("I is for
iris" and "Q is for quill"). After you read the name of the object, toddlers
may enjoy pointing it out in the picture. Preschoolers may enjoy determining the object themselves by reading the word and/or examining the
illustrations.

The great thing, too, about alphabet books is that they are easy to
make. With your help, your child can take photographs, draw pictures,

Here is the cover and a page from a child's self-made alphabet book.

and collect objects to fill the pages from A to Z! This is a time to be creative and think beyond the usual "A is for apple." *A* may be for your child's favorite Aunt Abby, *B* may be for Buddy, the family dog, and *C* may be for Carla, the next-door neighbor. One way to approach creating your own book includes the following steps:

* Have your child pick snapshots, magazine photos, and his own drawings of people, places and things.

* Write or have your child write (if he is able to) a letter (upper- and lowercase) on each page.

* Paste these clippings, photos, and drawings onto pages for the letter that they represent.

* Have your child help you put the pages together in order—such as by singing the alphabet song!

* Books can be laminated and bound together with string, metal fasteners, or binding—all of which can be done with the help of your local copy shop.

Here's one final suggestion for encouraging your child's exploration of letters and sounds: Use a tactile approach. Give your child opportunities to write letters in salt, sand, shaving cream, or gel. Have your child use her fingertips to write letters of the alphabet on your back. You have to guess which letter she has written. You can even guess the sound of the letter, too—just make sure she knows which you are saying, a sound of the letter or the letter name. You can switch, too, and you can have your child guess which letters you are writing on his back. This different spin on writing will help your child learn to form different letters, and young children often delight in this tactile approach to learning the alphabet.

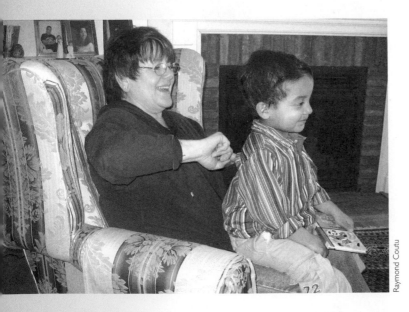

Raymond Coutu

Fifteen Fabulous Alphabet Books

Alphabet books come in all shapes, sizes, and types. Some tell stories; some convey information. Some are simple, containing only a single word for each letter; some are complex, devoting whole paragraphs to each letter. Reading a variety of alphabet books over time holds both children's interest and yours. Here are some old favorites and some brand-new winners. You'll have fun looking for your favorite!

ABC, Baby Me!
by S. B. Katz
Chronicling the daily lives of babies and their caregivers, this book captures the hearts of children and adults alike.

A, You're Adorable
by M. Alexander
This endearing alphabet book is based on the 1940s song of the same name. Children love the illustrations at any time of day, and the sweet message makes this a perfect alphabet book for bedtime.

Alpha Oops! The Day Z Went First
by A. Kontis
Just when you thought you could guess how an alphabet book might go, along comes this one! Z protests its placement at the end of the alphabet and demands that it have a chance to start things off ("Zebra and I are SICK of this last-in-line stuff!"). Enjoy this twist on the alphabet.

Alphabet City
by S. T. Johnson
Johnson embeds alphabet letters in realistic illustrations of city scenes. Children will have great fun finding and calling out the letters.

Alphabet Under Construction
by D. Fleming
Denise Fleming's colorful, playful, and just plain wonderful illustrations make this book ultra-engaging for toddlers and preschoolers.

Chicka Chicka Boom Boom
by B. Martin Jr. and J. Archambault
A classic! The letters of the alphabet crowd onto the top of a coconut tree. But . . . "Chicka chicka boom boom! Will there be enough room?" Children enjoy finding out through the playful rhyme and vivid illustrations.

Firefighters A to Z
by C. L. Demarest
The author of this book is a volunteer firefighter, and it shows! He goes beyond the usual things books tell us about firefighters to share some fascinating new concepts and vocabulary. A great book to use when children are engaged in dramatic play as firefighters.

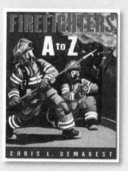

G Is for Goat
by P. Polacco
This board book captivates children with its illustrations from another time and place. Sparking many different emotions, children are excited by goats climbing and running, laugh at the goats munching on children's clothing instead of hay, and adore the baby goats, Zig, Zag, and Zoë.

Girls A to Z

by E. Bunting

This book depicts girls of different races, shapes, and sizes engaged in a variety of activities and careers—space exploration, ballet dancing, computer science—and ends with words of encouragement: "Be anything you want to be. Do what you want to do. Dream any dream you want to dream. The world is here for you."

The Hidden Alphabet

by L. Seeger

This is an engaging lift-the-flap guessing game, in which each letter is hidden from view; a word beginning with the hidden letter gives a hint at what to expect when you lift the flap. For example, the page for the letter *d* has a door on it. The page for the letter *o* depicts an olive. Some of the vocabulary will be familiar to most children, such as *egg*, *mouse*, and *toast*. Other words may be new, such as *inkblot* and *partridge*. All will be fun to guess.

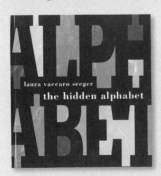

My First A B C Board Book

DK Publishing

Dorling Kindersley strikes again! The publisher of a number of wonderful books appropriate for infants, toddlers, and preschoolers offers this alphabet book featuring vivid photographs of everyday, and not so everyday, objects that begin with the target letter.

Q Is for Duck: An Alphabet Guessing Game

by M. Elting and M. Folsom

Q is for duck. Can you guess why? Because a duck says "Quack!" An interesting, highly appealing twist on alphabet books. Nearly every copy we've ever seen has been dog-eared.

Tomorrow's Alphabet

by G. Shannon

A stands for seed. Can you guess why? It's tomorrow's apple. This book really gets children thinking by exploring the concept of change from many angles. The book is excellent but challenging and, therefore, is appropriate for late preschoolers and kindergarteners.

The Underwater Alphabet Book

by J. Pallotta

Jerry Pallotta has written many wonderful informational alphabet books for children (which are usually best read over several sessions). In this book, alphabet letters are associated with underwater creatures: *H* is for Hammerhead Shark, *P* is for Porcupine Fish, and so on. Realistic illustrations and fascinating facts make it a winner for young children.

The Z Was Zapped: A Play in Twenty-Six Acts

by C. Van Allsburg

In this dramatic, black-and-white presentation of the alphabet, the Caldecott medalist depicts how each letter suffers a terrible mishap: "A was in an avalanche," "B was badly bitten," "C was cut to ribbons," and so forth. Not only is the book extremely entertaining, it's loaded with interesting vocabulary to discuss.

Vocabulary

Our vocabulary is composed of words we under-stand when reading and listening (receptive vocabulary) and/or use when writing and speaking (expressive vocabulary). Vocabulary is a major focus when educators think about literacy instruction, largely because studies have found a strong connection between vocabulary and later reading achievement.[78] As a parent, you probably won't use an instructional program to boost your child's vocabulary, but you can use some of the strategies suggested in them, especially when you read aloud. When you encounter a new word (for your child), you can do some or all of the following:

* Briefly explain what the word means; for example, when you come across the word *terrible* in *Where the Wild Things Are* by Maurice Sendak, you can say, "*Terrible*, that word means 'very bad' or 'awful.'"

* Have your child say the new word with you.

* Connect the new word's meaning to a word or words he already knows—for example, "You know the word *stegosaurus*, right? Well, *apatosaurus* is like that; it is the name of a kind of dinosaur."

* After reading aloud, revisit the new word. Later, use the new words in other situations. Your child will start to learn different ways of using certain words.[79]

Most of all, try to enjoy new words you encounter in read-alouds—words can sound interesting and be fun to say. New words are exciting for children to use themselves, and you may even be surprised about all of the words your child

What If a Text Contains Words or Ideas That I Find Offensive?

Not every text is written as we would like it to be. Some texts might include language that we find biased—whether it is related to gender, race, or ethnicity—or contain violent images. What should you do if you inadvertently encounter a book or website whose messages offend you? Although we do not know of any research about changing or editing text and whether that has an effect in any way, we would advise skipping over certain parts or editing wording, depending on the child to whom you are reading. For example, you might replace the word *fireman* with *firefighter* so you do not give your child the impression that only men can be firefighters. Very young children likely will not understand why we find certain words or images offensive, and therefore, don't worry about explaining why you are skipping over or editing text. For older children, such texts can provide opportunities for talk; you can explain, "The books says this . . . but we think this . . . Here's why . . ."

Books for Building World Knowledge

You can read:	To build knowledge about:
My First Word Board Book. DK Publishing	Words for all sorts of objects (infants, toddlers)
Baby Faces by M. Miller	Feelings (infants, toddlers)
Big Little by L. Patricelli	Part of a series on opposites (infants, toddlers)
Fuzzy Yellow Ducklings by M. Van Fleet	Shapes, colors, textures, animals (infants, toddlers)
Do You Have a Tail? by S. Taback	Animal characters (toddlers)
A Rainbow All Around Me by S. L. Pinkney	Colors, description (toddlers, preschoolers)
Piggies by A. Wood	Opposites (toddlers, preschoolers)
About Birds: A Guide for Children by C. Sill	Birds (preschoolers)
Hello Ocean by P. M. Ryan	Senses (preschoolers)
My Car by B. Barton	Cars, car parts (preschoolers)

remembers. Encourage your child to ask about unfamiliar words and praise her when she does so. Strive for a "word-curious" home.

World Knowledge

One great thing about reading is that it provides information about the world. World knowledge helps children comprehend all kinds of texts, such as books about dinosaurs and the solar system as well as recipes and letters. Read-alouds are a great way to build world knowledge. See Books for Building World Knowledge, at left, for suggestions of books to read and how they will build world knowledge.

Books are not the only source for learning about the world around us. Adults often read the newspaper in the kitchen as they drink their morning coffee or orange juice, and if you do this, you can keep your child up to date on things happening in the world around her. This can include reading aloud an article about an upcoming festival or parade in your area or events that might be happening nationally and beyond. There might be issues in the newspaper that you may not feel comfortable reading about to your child. Consider, though, explaining these types of events—natural disasters or major conflicts between countries—in your own words so that you can discuss them in developmentally appropriate ways with your child.

Studies have shown that one of the best ways to learn about the world around us is to connect books and other reading materials to hands-on experiences.[80] One approach, which many teachers use and research supports, is E-T-R.[81] It stands for Experience, Text, and Relationship. You can use the ideas behind E-T-R when you read aloud with your child.

E-T-R With Infants An example of using E-T-R with an infant involves using *Peek-a-Boo!* by Roberta Grobel Intrater, a book that features color photographs of babies and toddlers peeking at the camera with various expressions, props, and poses.

This child is making a connection between his ball and the photograph of the ball in the book.

E: Play peek-a-boo with the infant. While playing, say, "We are playing peek-a-boo."

T: Read *Peek-a-Boo!*, pronouncing the term "peek-a-boo" in the same way you did while playing peek-a-boo. Say, "The babies are playing peek-a-boo."

R: Explain, "The babies are playing peek-a-boo. We play peek-a-boo." Play peek-a-boo with the infant using props and terms from the book showing him pages that match your play.

E-T-R With Toddlers Here's an example of using E-T-R with a toddler using *The Best Book of Bugs* by Claire Llewellyn, a book that contains illustrations of and basic information about common insects such as ladybugs and flies.

E: Take your child on a quest for insects. Around and under logs and rocks and on or near trees and plants are good places to look. Collect insects in a container with air holes.

T: Return home to read Angela Royston's *Insects and Crawly Creatures* (or even consider reading it outside). Rather than reading the whole book, you might read only pages about insects you found or might have found.

R: Have your child compare the insects she found with those in the book. For example, if she found a ladybug, have her look at the photograph of a ladybug in the book and talk about similarities and differences between them. Read or reread the information about ladybugs so she can find out what food they eat, provide that food, and place it in the insect's container. (You might want to have an adult-level insect guide on hand for those uncommon or hard-to-identify insects.)

E-T-R With Preschoolers Finally, here is an example of an E-T-R with preschoolers using the book *Pop! A Book About Bubbles* by Kimberly Brubaker Bradley. This book provides a great deal of information about bubbles and activities your child can do with bubbles.

E: Provide your child with an opportunity to explore bubbles by giving him a hands-on activity, such as lathering up dish detergent in a plugged sink or tub or blowing bubbles outdoors. Talk with him about bubbles and encourage him to point out things he notices and wonders about.

T: Read *Pop! A Book About Bubbles*. As this book is too long to read in one sitting for most children, read those parts that relate most closely to things your child did, noticed, or wondered about during the "experience" phase.

R: Ask your child questions that relate his bubble play to the information in the book. "Did your bubbles do that?" "What happened when you tried this?" You may want to return to the "experience" phase to give your child time to experience what he has learned from the book and make more connections.

Comprehension

Comprehension, the ability to construct meaning with text that is read aloud, or that one reads oneself, is the purpose of reading. When you read aloud, don't read the book straight through without stopping. Rather, encourage your child's comprehension by doing the following:

* Allow your child to ask questions and ask your child questions as you read.

* Ask questions that go beyond simple "yes" or "no," right or wrong answers. Try questions that will really get your child thinking (i.e., higher-order thinking). Begin questions with "Why do you think . . ." "Tell me what you think about . . ." etc. Ask "What does this remind you of?" and "What do you think will happen next?" (See the chart on pages 148–149 for additional comments and questions.) Even though lots of interaction during a read-aloud is good, do not attempt all of these questions or comments in one reading; you don't want to ask so many questions or make so many comments that it interrupts the flow of the reading. Doing that may make the reading hard to follow and frustrate your child.

* Have a real conversation about the book, in which both you and your child are trying to understand its meaning together.[82] Remember that often there can be more than one interpretation of a text.

* Help your child make connections between the book and his own life.

Engaging in these activities will help your child develop important literacy skills, habits, and knowledge, all of which he can carry to the next book read and beyond.

As we mentioned earlier, reading aloud with your child should happen frequently *and* should be enjoyable. And remember that during this time, your child will be developing vital skills and knowledge as well as a love of literacy.

What to Focus on and What to Say During Read-Alouds to Build Comprehension

Comprehension skill:	Examples of what to say while reading:	Especially good to use when . . .
Identify Factual Details	Where does this story take place? What is the name of a baby goat?	the detail is important to understanding the text.
Reading Between the Lines	Why did the boy run back home? Why do mice avoid snakes?	the text does not ask the question directly, but the answer is important.
Forming Opinions	What do you think they should do? What's your opinion on this?	there is a potential for many different answers.
Bridging to Experience	Have you ever had a fight with your brother? Have you . . .	text content may relate to the child's experiences.
Predicting	What do you think will happen next? What will the author tell about next?	emphasizing reading for purpose or understanding text structure.
Focusing on Text Structure	What is the problem for this boy? How are dogs and cats the same and different?	teaching story structure or an informational text structure such as compare/contrast.
Labeling	Do you know what that is called? What does . . . mean?	focusing on developing the child's vocabulary.
Making Connections Between Books	Does that remind you of another book we have read?	text or content is similar to something else you have read.
Linking to Writing	Is there anything there we can use in our writing? Let's remember . . .	text relates closely to a writing project.
Adopting Authorship	If you were the author, how would you end the story?	focusing on teaching child to think like an author.
Evaluating	Did you find that funny? I didn't like the way that . . .	the child is not evaluating text spontaneously.
Pointing Out	Look at that fox hidden there. Look at how the print is larger.	the child is unlikely to notice important details on her own.
Explaining	These are what the water comes through. A buffet is . . .	dealing with an unfamiliar word, concept, plot, etc.
Summarizing	So what was this whole part of the book about?	teaching your child to sum up, synthesize.

Types of Talk

Here are some types of talk about texts that will build comprehension during read-alouds, and some sample situations of when each type of talk may be useful:

Type of talk:	Explanation/example:	Especially good to use when . . .
Chiming in	Your child reads part of the text along with you.	text is very familiar or predictable.
Elaborating	Child makes a comment like "Yuck," and you elaborate on it.	there's more to say related to the comment.
Giving feedback	Child makes comment, and you affirm it: "Yes, I think so, too."	encouraging the child to comment on the text.
Managing	Let's go on to the next page now. Let's go back and read again.	the child is not sure of what you are doing.

(Some categories adapted from Neuman, 1996)[83]

Collaborative Productions

Dramatic Play:
Another Avenue Into Literacy

Julia is a tour guide, leading visitors through noteworthy sites. Ababu is a butterfly joyously fluttering from flower to flower in the garden. Joseph is the Cat in the Hat, visiting Sally and her brother on "that cold, cold wet day." Few experiences are more delightful to parents than watching their children engage in imaginary play. Pretending to be someone (or something) else, though, isn't just for fun—it's essential for language and literacy growth! It provides opportunities to expand children's vocabulary, build knowledge of the world, explore print in lifelike situations, and more. Taking on "roles" can involve using literacy props, such as a waiter with a menu or a shopper with a grocery list, which provides reading and writing practice using a variety of texts. It also develops an understanding of functional literacy, that is, coming to realize that literacy serves different purposes in our lives—to entertain, to inform, to persuade, to report, and so forth. As adults, we use literacy to accomplish tasks every day, and dramatic play allows children to do that as well.

Ellen Daugherty Durr

What Is
Dramatic Play?

When your child is given a phone, pad of paper, and pencil, does she begin to play office? Does your child use a blanket as a cape to become a superhero? Dramatic play involves pretending—some people even refer to it as pretend play or dress-up. As we mentioned, when a child engages in dramatic play, she is taking on a role and may incorporate different materials (or props) to carry out this role. When dramatic play incorporates literacy, a child will:

* See and explore how different types of texts can be used

* Discover that she needs different kinds of texts to accomplish different kinds of tasks (think about the texts a doctor uses as opposed to a cashier)

* Create different kinds of text, from signs and receipts to labels and lists, to get things done

* Learn and use the structure and parts of stories when she pretends to be a familiar storybook character (for example, recreating the plot of how a girl goes from sweeping cinders to becoming a princess wearing glass slippers)

As adults, we read and write for real purposes. We use our literacy skills in many different ways, and children can, too, as they engage in dramatic play that incorporates literacy-related props.

What to Use in Dramatic Play

You can enhance your child's dramatic play by supplying her with materials and literacy-related props. And supplying the right kinds of materials and props starts with thinking about the type of play in which your child wants to engage. For example, many young children enjoy playing house. Some typical house-playing materials include a stove, refrigerator, baby dolls, chairs and tables, baby supplies, and a mailbox. Literacy-related props might include newspapers, children's books, baby/parenting magazines, paper and pencils, shopping ads, slim paper for list making, coupons, magnetic letters for the fridge, signs like "There's no place like home" and "Welcome," photo albums with captions, and letters in the mailbox.

DRAMATIC PLAY

If your child wants to play restaurant, you may provide him with play food, aprons, a chef's hat, dishes, vases with flowers, tables set for dining, play money, a cash register, dress-up clothes, and other items. Literacy-related props for playing restaurant might include menus, cookbooks, signs for the restaurant, a chalkboard or dry-erase board to list "specials," order pads, pencils, and more. (See Ideas for Themes and Literacy Props in Dramatic Play on pages 154–155 for more ideas.)

And that's only the beginning. Whatever your child's play theme, take some time to think of materials and literacy-related props that could be included in the play. You might want to come up with your own list of themes for your child to consider, along with the right materials and props to go along with those themes.

How to Introduce Props in Dramatic Play

Once your child has decided upon a theme, and you've gathered the right materials and literacy-related props, the next step is to think about what to do with the props. You can help your child by introducing him to the prop by saying something like, "Here's an order pad in case you want to write down our breakfast order." Think about ways to model how to use the props, too. If you and your child are "camping out," you might refer to a guide book about birds as you look through binoculars in search of wildlife. If you set up a veterinary clinic, you might model how to read a magazine as you and your animal wait to be seen, or write a prescription after the animal's examination.

Look for common items around your home that relate somehow to play themes in which your child is interested or books that you and your child have read together. For example, breakfast bowls might remind you of *Goldilocks and the Three Bears*, and you can point this out to your child by saying, "Look, these three bowls make me think of the bowls of porridge in *Goldilocks and the Three Bears*." This might be all it takes to jump-start pretend play based on that story.

Your child may surprise you by using materials and props in ways for which they are unintended—for example, a drumstick may become a magic wand, a menu may become fairy wings, a colander a construction helmet—and that is perfectly okay! Such inventiveness is evidence of your child's imagination at work. She may also use props across play boundaries, such as using a grocery store coupon as a movie ticket. That's okay, too. As a rule of thumb, show your child typical ways to use materials and props, but also leave room for the creative uses she thinks up.

Are Babies Too Young for Dramatic Play?

Babies, of course, don't play with props in the same way that older children do. They do, however, engage in their own form of dramatic play—they mimic the sounds, gestures, and facial expressions we make. Provide nonbreakable mirrors near the changing table and on the floor at crawling level to support and promote mimicking. Make faces in the mirror with the baby. And, if you like, sing silly songs. Babies will not only learn facial expressions but also the rhythms they hear in the songs. Providing objects babies associate with particular movements may also encourage their play. For example, a baby may move a spatula around a pan the way he has seen his parents do, insert play keys into a toy truck as if starting the ignition, or raise a play telephone up to his ear and babble into it.

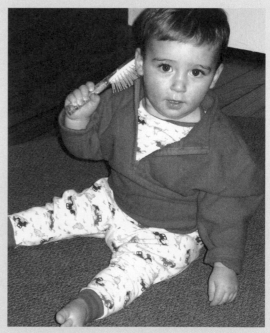

David Ammer

Ideas for Themes and Literacy Props in Dramatic Play

Dramatic Play Themes and Props	Literacy Props
House stove, refrigerator, babies, chairs and tables, dishes, baby supplies, mailbox	Newspapers, children's books, baby/parenting magazines, paper and pencils, shopping ads, slim paper for list making, coupons, magnetic letters for fridge, signs (e.g. "There's no place like home" and "Welcome"), photo albums with captions, letters in mailbox
Boat shape of boat taped onto the floor, with kitchen area (galley), chairs for fishing, fishing poles, life jackets, binoculars	Maps of lakes, fish field guides, posters of different types of fish, fishing magazines, *Ranger Rick*, *Big Backyard*, or *Wild Animal Baby* magazines
Airplane windows that look out onto clouds, chairs in rows, headsets for pilots, steering wheel for pilot and copilot (can be just circles of cardboard affixed to box with brads), small overnight suitcases with dress-up clothes, pretend food and dishes. Create a galley by placing a play refrigerator and stove between the "cockpit" and the seating area.	Travel brochures (available for free from travel agencies), maps, flight manual (real or made-up), order pad and pencils for flight attendants, advertising posters with slogans like "Fly the friendly skies," flight safety cards, in-flight magazines available from airlines, name tags, tickets, passports
Grocery Store tables/shelves, small grocery carts, cash register, money, purses, wallets, brown bags (not plastic for safety reasons)	Signs for shelves, coupons, grocery store ads from newspaper, posters of different foods, empty containers of foods or other products with labels, sale posters
Veterinary Clinic stuffed animals, medical equipment (such as stethoscopes, gauze, and shotters), white doctor coats or small, white adult dress shirts	Charts of animals, books on animals (e.g DK's books *Dogs* or *Cats*), pet care books, magazines for the waiting room area, boxes labeled "medicine" (Don't use bottles or real medicine packages as we don't want children thinking that getting into those is a good idea.), appointment book, medical charts, file folders with paper and pencil
Campsite tent, stuffed animals (or "fossils" depending on theme), binoculars, pretend fire, play food, dishes, small picnic table, sleeping bags	Wildlife posters (available free from your state's Department of Natural Resources), field guides or books on birds (or mammals, dinosaurs, etc., depending on the theme)
Submarine large piece of cardboard (appliance box, cut open) with portholes cut in side, steering wheel, periscope, pictures of fish or other underwater creatures, blue tulle or crepe paper draped from ceiling, green crepe paper draped from ceiling for seaweed, diving masks, flippers	Guidebooks on fish, informational books on underwater life, and posters with text about life underwater
Ice Cream Parlor dishes, cones made from paper, spoons, table and chairs, tubs of "ice cream" (yarn pom-poms in a variety of colors), ice cream scoops, money, cash register, aprons	Order forms and pencils, poster of flavor choices, price poster, store sign, labels on flavor buckets, empty containers of chocolate sauce, butterscotch, or cherry toppings with labels

Firehouse phone, hoses, fire truck created from box, climber, or lined up chairs, coats, rubber boots, fire hats, extinguisher (can be oatmeal can covered in red paper with piece of hose attached)	Map of city, poster of the order in which to put on gear, fire safety posters, paper and pencil for taking phone messages
Flower Shop tub with potting soil, plastic pots, artificial flowers, phone, cash register, money, shovels, plastic vases, refrigerator for floral arrangements, ribbon	Seed packets with labels, posters of plants, FTD book (get an old one from your local florist), FTD calendar (free from florist), sticks with names of plants on them, order forms and pencils
Bakery flour in a tub, natural-colored play dough (and tons of it!), cookie cutters, rolling pins, pans, oven, sink, aprons, oven mitts, phone, cash register, money, boxes decorated to look like cakes	Bakery sign, price lists, labels on shelves of baked goods, order forms, pencils, recipe cards, cookbooks, paper for children to label their creations
Pizza Parlor felt pieces in white and red to make pizza and sauce, felt pieces cut to look like cheese, pepperoni, mushrooms, green pepper (each in its own container for sorting), oven, oven mitts, phone, cash register, money, table for eating "in," dishes, aprons	Order forms, pencils, pizza cookbook, menus, signs advertising the daily special

Other themes include bookshop, zoo, space ship, train, and baby hospital. You might also try ideas inspired by a read-aloud. For example, Susan once put a children's pool filled with straw in her dramatic play area when she was teaching. After reading *Make Way for Ducklings* by Robert McCloskey, the children reenacted that story. At one point, a little girl stood up and announced, "I can't fly . . . I'm molting!" Dramatic play became a forum for retelling, chewing on the ideas in the text, and fully comprehending them. Regardless of what inspires themes, dramatic play can contribute to children's literacy if it is designed with literacy in mind.

Why Dramatic Play Matters

Play is a powerful tool children use throughout childhood to learn about their world.[84] In its 2009 position statement, the National Association for the Education of Young Children strongly calls for providing children with play-based experiences. We also know that such experiences can yield academic benefits when children enter school.[85] In addition to more general benefits, there are specific aspects of language and literacy that can be developed through rich dramatic play:

* Acting out stories, a form of retelling, can lead to greater comprehension. Additionally, play scenarios can be influenced by informative texts. (At Susan's house, her boys played Shark Attack regularly after learning how sharks bump into their prey before attacking. Deciding who was prey and who was shark made for some lively problem-solving opportunities, too!)

* Pretending and role playing involving new situations can introduce and reinforce new vocabulary associated with the play. For example, if a child is playing grocery store, she can use the words "scan," "sale," "display," "checkout," and "produce"—and the adults playing along can introduce and use those words, too.

* Social relationships and scenarios, and the problem-solving language necessary to maintain those relationships, can play out in pretend play. For example, a child may take care of a baby doll and repeat language he heard his parents use when talking to him, or a child may reenact a trip to the emergency room using the language of that environment, including the reassuring words she heard nurses and parents using.

* Dramatic play provides opportunities for children to engage in literacy activities that they've observed in everyday life, such as writing messages, reading maps, making road signs for truck play, or making grocery lists for their pretend grocery store.

The potential benefits are extensive. One recent study found that pretend play between children and their parents can advance language development for children with special needs and typically developing children alike.[86] The best part of dramatic play is how engaging it can be for both children and their adult play partners. (See pages 150–155 for lots of ideas for maximizing this wonderful type of play with your child.)

Blocks and Puzzles: Building Literacy With Toys

When we introduced you to Trevor at the start of this chapter, we highlighted a few toys that you would find in his bedroom, including blocks and puzzles. In this last section, we discuss block and puzzle play, which connects thinking and doing, as little hands, mouths, and eyes investigate, assemble, and experiment. Interacting with blocks and puzzles can help build literacy, especially when print is involved.

Blocks

Blocks of different shapes, sizes, and colors are a mainstay in many children's bedrooms. So use them to promote literacy. Here are a couple of ideas. Use alphabet blocks to talk about letter names and letter sounds. You might also ask your child to record block constructions on a piece of paper or in a journal or to take photographs of them. Around the picture, your child can label elements of it in whatever writing form he is most comfortable.

Also consider making available construction-related books such as *Albert's Alphabet* by Leslie Tryon, *Block City*

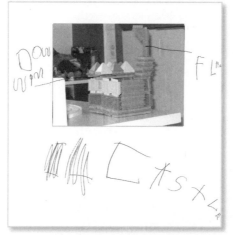

This child documented the castle she created by placing a photograph of it on paper and labeling a window and flag.

Robert Louis Stevenson's poem illustrated by Daniel Kirk, and *Architecture Shapes* by Michael J. Crosbie and Steve Rosenthal. Books such as these will inspire little builders

Using Different Puzzles to Promote Literacy

You can use:	To help your child:
Alphabet puzzles	Learn the letters of the alphabet and orientation of letters
Puzzles with words and pictures	Learn about print, how words are spelled, and what words mean (e.g., the word and the picture *airplane* are paired together on a piece)
Puzzles with characters or scenes from books	Learn to retell stories and have conversations about characters and scenes that they see on the puzzle

David Ammer

with their vivid photographs of buildings, elements of buildings, and related print.

Puzzles

Puzzles are another great tool for building literacy because some puzzles require children to match pictures and labels—for example, the child may have to insert a car-shaped piece into a slot labeled "car" or assemble pieces with labeled pictures, as with the puzzle shown in the photograph at left.

Furthermore, as they construct puzzles, children must think about "orientation"—that is, the way each piece must be rotated in order to fit—which is excellent preparation for writing alphabet letters. Just like puzzle pieces, letters must be oriented a certain way or, more times than not, they won't make sense. For example, when you turn the letter *M* upside down, it becomes a *W*, and when you rotate a *d*, you can get a *p*. So how do puzzles help? They require children to test the direction of pieces and look closely at how different pieces fit together to form a big picture. This is just what children have to do with letters when they write.

Concluding Thoughts

Your child's bedroom is brimming with possibilities for promoting literacy. Reading aloud is an obvious activity, and we hope we've given you some fresh ideas for that in this chapter. Perhaps not as obvious, however, is integrating literacy into pretend play—but with some thought, you will find how nicely dramatic play and literacy come together. Finally, the toys that tend to fill a child's bedroom can also be used to boost his or her reading and writing development, in addition to providing great fun for little ones.

The Power of Labeling: Build Literacy as You Organize Toys, Clothing, and Other Essentials

In addition to posters and books, you can include even more print in your child's bedroom *and* keep it organized by labeling toy bins and clothing drawers, to name just two areas ripe for labeling. When you organize with labels, your child not only learns about the importance of cleaning up, but she also comes to see that her belongings have names that can be represented in writing. Start by labeling with pictures *and* print—for example, write the word *trucks* and put a picture of a truck on the storage container for trucks. Or use print and picture labels to help your child sort and put away pants, shorts, and underwear in the correct drawers. By doing this, your child will start to associate words with the things they represent. As she gains more familiarity with reading and writing, you can use print alone to label items in the bedroom.

But don't stop at labeling—be sure to encourage interaction with labels. Specifically, introduce labels to your child and show him how to use them. For example, when it's time to clean up before dinner, show him how to find the bin for dolls by pointing to the label on the bin. Putting away clothing, too, is another occasion for modeling how to use labels to keep things organized in the bedroom.

Meagan Shedd

CHAPTER 7

Literacy in Unexpected Places

Raymond Coutu

When you are changing the sixth diaper of the day, literacy is probably the last thing on your mind (unless you're daydreaming about the exotic setting of the novel you're reading or more likely, planning to read . . . someday). If you don't connect diaper changes with literacy, it's understandable, but such an encounter might be a missed opportunity. Diapering time, bath time, clean-up time, and snack time are great moments to sneak in literacy experiences. As we indicated in Chapter 2, encounters with literacy can and should be available to your child throughout the day. . . even in the least expected places. In this chapter, we offer suggestions for building literacy during two very common activities—using the bathroom and doing laundry—and to deal with two very common "sticky points" for all parents and their children, waiting and transitioning.

Using the Bathroom

Let's face it, kids are interested in bathrooms and everything we do in them. Most children like to play in the tub. Others could set up residence on the throne. Still others like to brush their teeth and wash their hands. In some families, the bathroom is as busy as the kitchen. So take advantage of this time and use it as "literacy central." Here are a few ideas to get you started.

The Loo Library

Many adults read in the bathroom. Consider making it easier for children to do that, too, by adding a small basket of books they can peruse while on the potty. For the young and unsteady aimer, use laminated or plastic-coated books for easy cleanup. Children's magazines are a great choice, too, because they are less costly than books if they are ruined. And, chances are, they will be ruined!

Meagan Shedd

Brushing Up on Literacy

Hang a chart in your bathroom that illustrates the steps for your child's morning routine, such as brushing teeth, getting dressed, combing hair, and whatever else he typically does. Write the text next to each picture so that you can talk about it as you carry out each step with your child. Charts like this can be created to help him carry out the steps himself, too—for example, how to brush teeth, how to wash hands, and how to get dressed. Again, make sure you have both picture and text for each step.

Tub Talk

Bath time can be a wonderful time of the day in your home, as your child winds down for bedtime. The water is soothing and has interesting properties. Bath time is a great time to do all of the following activities.

* Talk together about the day.

* Explore new vocabulary, such as *sink*, *float*, and *suspend*.

* Offer cups and other containers and talk about mathematical concepts such as *more*, *less*, *same*, and *equal*.

* Take advantage of the captive audience and share a book about bathtime, or another water-related topic, such as *Clifford's Bathtime* by Norman Bridwell, *Tub People* by Pam Conrad, *Five Minutes' Peace* by Jill Murphy, and *My Water Comes From the Rocky Mountains* by Tiffany Fourment. For the more daring, try Mary Cerullo's *The Truth About Great White Sharks* or *Whales* by Gail Gibbons.

* Paint and write on the wall with shaving cream tinted with food coloring. (Be sure to avoid mentholated cream, however, as that can sting.) Commercially prepared tub paints and crayons are also available. Encourage your child to tell you about the pictures and writing he creates. Make sure the artist signs his work!

* Encourage pretend play. Follow your child's lead as she becomes a mermaid or a fish. Talk about her imaginary life as that creature. What does she do all day? What might she do at night? What does she eat? Encourage her to use her imagination to think like a scientist. Ask her what she wonders about. You might later read books about sea life to find some of the answers. (Good luck explaining the mermaid!)

* After reading a book together about boats (such as *Boats* by Byron Barton or *Boats* by Anne Rockwell), and before bathtime, see if you and your child can create something that might work as a toy boat. Use materials you have around the house, such as plastic soda bottles, milk cartons, and bars of soap for hulls; straws and popsicle sticks for masts; and handkerchiefs for sails. Make a couple of different kinds of boats and have your child predict which will stay afloat the longest.

BATHROOM TIME

Doing Laundry

You may not be thinking much about literacy when sorting dirty clothes, shoveling wet clothes into the dryer, or putting away piles of clean laundry, but your youngster could be learning new concepts from these mundane activities. Here's how.

Amazing Attributes

While you are sifting through your next mountain of laundry, have your little one help you figure out the pile into which each article of clothing goes by pointing out the similarities and differences among the items. For example, hold up a gym sock and say, "I need to put this in the whites pile. Help me find other clothes that are white." Or, "I try to wash all the jeans in one load. Help me find all the jeans in this pile. They are all blue. How many can you find?" This kind of talk may help children better understand how things are similar and different. (If you want to expand this understanding through books, try *Big and Little* by Steve Jenkins, which compares and contrasts related animals of different sizes, such as a hummingbird and an ostrich; or *Are Trees Alive?* by Debbie S. Miller, which compares trees and humans.) Talking about attributes also expands children's understanding of concepts (size, colors, and shapes), and helps them make connections between seemingly unlike things (Daddy's white shirt and the baby's white bib are both white, but they are different in size, function, and the number of stains!).

Folding Phonics

Susan doesn't mind folding clothes at her house, but she really hates putting them away. So she sorts clothes into family member piles as she folds them, and then individual family members put their piles away. An easy way to include a child in this project (beyond putting their own clothes away) is to have him place the folded item into the correct pile. The directions would go something like "This shirt belongs to Daddy. Can you find Daddy's pile?" In addition to building sorting skills, you can build phonemic awareness skills by saying something like, "This shirt belongs to someone whose name starts with the /d/ sound. Can

you find that person's pile?" Of course, it could be Daddy or Dawson in Susan's family, and that necessitates looking at other attributes (see Amazing Attributes above) and discussing those. This activity can be extended to include delivering lunches to older kids, choosing items at the store, sorting the mail, and so forth.

As children become more aware of letter names, you can say, "These jeans belong to the person whose name starts with *t* (this time saying the name of the letter). To build letter recognition (identifying the letter by sight), you might put the letter in front of the pile. Variation from time to time keeps it interesting. You could even switch to sorting by the last sound or letter in someone's name if your child is particularly sound-savvy—for example, "Find the pile for the person whose name ends in the /m/ sound."

LAUNDRY TIME

Waiting Without Worry

As adults, we find ourselves in an endless stream of waiting situations: waiting for the cable guy, for the important phone call, for the banana bread to finish baking, for the library to open on a rainy Saturday morning. Children tend to act out when they are not engaged. And how can we expect them to be engaged when they are following us around on various errands, doing activities as interesting as watching paint dry? So, anticipate their boredom (and subsequent undesirable behavior) and give them some of the following mind- and literacy-building activities.

I Spy

Build your child's vocabulary and her ability to make connections at the same time with this simple game. You likely played this as a child yourself, but to refresh your memory, the rules call for one person ("the spier") to give a clue about an object that she identifies, such as "I spy something blue," and the other person ("the guesser") to look around and locate the object based on that clue. (At first, to save your sanity, you may always want to be the spier since children tend to change what they are spying without letting the guesser know!) To make the game more literacy focused, try:

* I spy something sticky (gooey, hot, cold, furry, etc.).
  (Builds vocabulary)

* I spy something that starts with the /s/ sound.
  (Builds phonemic awareness)

* I spy something that starts with the letter *f*.
  (Builds letter-identification skills)

* I spy something that rhymes with *cat*.
  (Builds phonological awareness)

* I spy something that is the opposite of soft.
  (Builds conceptual skills)

* I spy something that is spelled p-o-t. (Builds spelling skills)

Get creative. You can easily modify this game for any child over 2 years old, and some children under 2. With very young children, you can name the objects themselves: "I spy a chair. Point to a chair." I Spy can be played nearly anytime, anywhere.

Twenty Questions

Most young children have a hard time forming questions, so this old game is best played with at least one additional adult or older child to provide assistance. Basically, this is a guessing game in which one person chooses a mystery person or item and the rest of group asks yes-or-no questions until one group member figures out what the item is. To start, you might say, "I'm thinking of an animal. You can ask me about it and see if you can guess what kind of an animal it is." Let the child ask questions and guess, and then invite her to choose an item. (As with I Spy, if the child switches items midstream, consider choosing items yourself until the child has a better grasp of the game—or, better yet, have her secretly draw the item, write its first letter, or have another adult draw or write it, which makes it more difficult to switch mid-game.) By asking questions about the mystery items, children get better at categorizing and grouping. After all, it takes a long time and wastes a lot of guesses if children start asking about every animal that comes to mind, one at a time. A more effective strategy that can be modeled for them is sorting the options into categories—or engaging in categorical thinking. Here's an example:

* Is it a fish? No.

* Does it have legs? Yes.

* Does it have feathers? Yes.

* Does it live in the woods? No.

* Does it live on a farm? Yes.

* Is it a rooster? Yes!

If children seem to be stumped, a recap can sometimes help. "Well, we figured out that it is brown, it has fur, it lives in the woods, and it eats fish. Do you have an idea what it might be?" You can also give additional

WAITING TIME

clues if needed: "This animal starts with a /l/ sound." Or, "This animal makes the sound 'meow.'"

It may surprise you that even young children can start to group animals (and items) in this way if adults show them how. Our own children started asking about whether certain animals were mammals when they were just preschoolers. Again, this example shows if you give kids good vocabulary and link it to concepts, they'll use that information to extend their knowledge!

Categories

As quickly as you can, name ten items you can find in a kitchen! Categories is another wonderful game for developing and strengthening vocabulary as well as world knowledge. Players take turns naming a category. Then everyone works together to name at least 10 items in that category. If you get to 10 items quickly for a given category, you can strive for 15 or even 20 items! Here are 10 different categories you might use in the game (x10 each = 100 items!):

* Colors
* Breakfast foods
* Holidays
* Sports
* Animals you might see at a zoo
  (or on a farm, in a forest, in a desert, and so on)
* Plants we eat
* Types of bugs
* Kinds of furniture
* Things we do every day
* Ways we can get from place to place

As you play, explain items that may be unfamiliar to children. Praise children's efforts to think of items, especially when they have thought hard to come up with them. Consider keeping records of achievements, such as the most items the family has collectively named for one category, or the greatest number of categories a family has completed in one day.

Transitioning Without Trauma

Whether they're going from blocks to bed or from Grandma's to the grocery store, many children have a hard time transitioning from one activity to another, which is understandable. After all, being asked to stop in the middle of doing something without warning isn't pleasant for anyone, young or old. Giving children warnings can help (e.g., "You have 5 more minutes to play before we get ready to go to the library"). This section will also supply you with other ideas that can help your child feel more in control of his activities and promote a growing sense of self-sufficiency.

What's Your Sign?

In some schools, teachers use signs to help children transition from one activity to the next. A five-minute-warning sign helps children know to wind down their play and get ready for the next activity. You may not feel the need to be so formal at home, but this is a print-based way to give your child a silent warning. When you hold up your hand at the park to let him know he had five more minutes to play, you encourage him to "read" the symbol of your splayed fingers. And, of course, reading sign language is a literacy activity.

**A child-made sign that says,
"Don't come in, please!!!"**

Everywhere a Sign

Some families post signs to remind kids to flush the toilet, take off their shoes upon entering the home, and carry out other tasks that help the household run smoothly. Reminders you hear yourself giving your children repeatedly are good candidates for posting on signs. Ask your child what signs she thinks you should make and have her help post them.

Message in a Basket

You can also avoid transition traumas by giving your child opportunities to accomplish tasks on her own, such as getting her own snack. Here's one way to do that. Have a basket full of crackers and if, for example, you only want children to take three at a time, clip a sign to the basket with the numeral "3," the word "three," and three dots, so your child knows how many to take. You don't have to stand over your child making sure she counts out the right amount, and she'll appreciate the opportunity to do this for herself. Of course, counting together and reading the signs together, at least at first, is a great way to talk about those symbols and what they mean.

You can also use pictures when you make recipes together and introduce your child to how-to texts by laying out the steps of a recipe for your child to follow, such as:

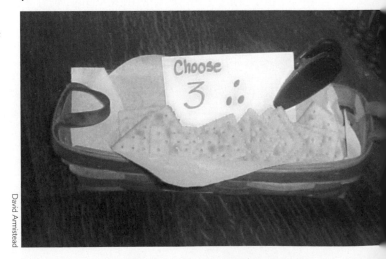

David Armistead

Picture #1 Wash your hands.

Picture #2 Pour pudding mix into a bowl.

Picture #3 Measure 1 cup of milk.

Picture #4 Pour the milk into the mix.

Picture #5 Stir.

Picture #6 Refrigerate for five minutes.

Picture #7 EAT!

A great book that uses picto-recipes is *Cup Cooking* by Barbara Johnson Foote. Children love to eat what they have made, and what a yummy way to introduce a child to following directions! (For more on this recipe and for specific snack recipes, see Chapter 4.)

Concluding Thoughts

You are already doing so much with your child. With minimal effort, you can turn your everyday tasks into rich learning opportunities. Not only will this provide practice for developing literacy, but in many cases, it will also provide you with peace of mind because your child will be engaged more frequently. "I'm bored" can become "Can we play again?"

CHAPTER 8

Literacy Beyond the Home

Jin Xiuzhan

Dorothy may have mused, "There's no place like home," but being away from home is a big part of most of our lives. Whether running errands, shuttling children back and forth to activities, or heading off for family vacations, we spend lots of time out and about. So we can't afford to neglect literacy during this time, and, fortunately, we don't have to—there are many exciting ways to expand literacy beyond the home.

This chapter shows you how to promote literacy in a variety of locations:

* In restaurants

* On errands

* In the car, on a bus, on a train, and on a plane

* In the great outdoors

* At the library and bookstore

By the time you've finished reading the chapter, you will have many new ideas for making your out-and-about time burst with literacy!

Literacy in Restaurants

Despite the fact that we might hope for a nice home-cooked meal every night of the week, many of us find ourselves in restaurants on a regular basis. And no matter how family-friendly the establishment may be, eating out often means some waiting, sometimes a lot of waiting, with antsy, hungry children—children who need to be entertained. So why not fold in a bit of literacy?

Because Nell's cooking skills range from boiling water to, well, boiling water, she takes her family out to eat *a lot*. So she has practiced both tried-and-true and inventive activities to keep children busy until their meals arrive. These are her favorites.

Place Your Order

Let children know their choices for food and drink, and ask them what they'd like. Read, rather than tell, children their options from the menu, pointing to the print as you read. Suggest children circle their choice with their finger or write it on a piece of paper.

Play Restaurant in the Restaurant

Many children enjoy playing restaurant, and that play does not need to take place in the home or child care setting. It can take place in actual restaurants. In fact, playing restaurant in a restaurant can lend an exciting element of authenticity to your child's play. Bringing along a small pad of paper and writing instrument (we always keep both in our purses!) allows children to take your order. The restaurant's menus and table settings can also work into the play. Children may enjoy "serving" you the bread, salt, and pepper. They may also enjoy providing a "prize" for a younger sibling at the end of the meal, such as a ghost made of a napkin or a drawing on the back of receipt, just as some real restaurants do.

Pass Notes

One challenge we face at restaurants, particularly when dining out with other adults, is how to interact with our children while also holding a conversation with those adults. One answer to this is to pass notes. Have children draw and/or write what they want to tell you while you are talking with the grown-ups. Then take a moment from your conversation to read their message and write back to them. If your child is not able to read your note, read it to him. He may appreciate the help. For example, you could write:

Did you have a good day?   ☐ Yes   ☐ No

Who did you play with today?   ☐ Ben   ☐ Dante   ☐ Juan   ☐ Sarah

What do you want for dessert?   ☐ Ice cream   ☐ Pie   ☐ Cookie

Can you draw something you did at school today?

Of course, at some point, your notes should be followed up with discussion—we don't want to reduce our check-ins about our children's day to one-word responses! But passing notes is an engaging and literacy-enriched way to do some communicating during a busy dinner.

Have Fun With Sugar Packets

We told you we're inventive! Actually, Nell's daughter had great fun in years past with sugar packets. She arranged them to make alphabet letters or pictures. She hid little notes (such as "M for Mom") under individual packets, and her parents' job was to guess which packet had "their" note under it. Sugar packets are also great for counting syllables or sounds in words. (See Chapter 5 for more information on counting syllables and sounds in words.) Similarly, jelly packets are great for those activities, as well as for identifying colors and sorting by color. Sugar and jelly packets have helped us pass hours in restaurants—how sweet it is!

Read Books

While waiting for your meals to arrive, why not squeeze in a read-aloud? Any kind of book is appropriate, especially one of the many wonderful children's books on or related to food or food preparation. During a trip to a pizza parlor, you might read *Pete's a Pizza* by William Steig with your infant, toddler, or younger preschooler, or *The Little Red Hen (Makes a Pizza)* by Philemon Sturges with your older preschooler. Here are three more:

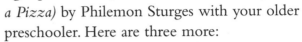

* *One Hungry Monster: A Counting Book in Rhyme* by S. H. O'Keefe. (toddler, younger preschooler)

* *If You Give a Pig a Pancake* by L. Numeroff. (younger or older preschooler)

* *Feast for 10* by C. Falwell. (younger or older preschooler)

Children often enjoy making connections between what's happening in the book and what's happening around them, and making connections provides many opportunities for developing literacy, as we explain later in this chapter.

Draw and Write

Of course, as you know, some restaurants provide crayons and disposable menus with child-friendly activities printed on them. If your child is interested in these activities, fine. But be aware that these are often not designed for children birth to 5 years old, and if your child is ready for them, she

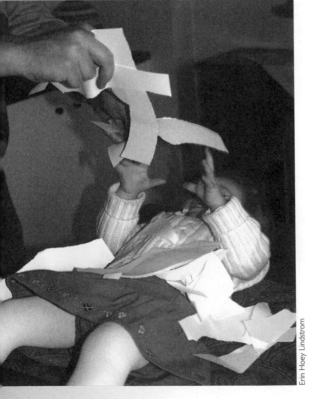

Erin Hoey Lindstrom

It's great fun to act out *Pete's a Pizza* at home. Here the parent is sprinkling "cheese" on the "pizza."

most likely needs more space to write than the menu provides. So we suggest traveling to restaurants with some paper and other writing materials of your own. Or, if there are paper placemats, most servers will gladly provide extras so your child can use the back. (See Diaper Bag Essentials, to the right.)

Play Games

Games like Twenty Questions, I Spy, and Categories, which are discussed on pages 166–168, are both great ways to develop literacy and keep children busy in restaurants.

Play With Words

Many of the word games for the living room that we discuss in Chapter 5, such as Going on Vacation, Guess What I'm Saying, and Who Gets Up?, work well in restaurants, too. Another game is the Describing Game. You might pose questions like *What is the stickiest item at the table? What is the most delicious? The healthiest?* After a while, your child will most likely pose questions like these herself. The game invites everyone at the table to give an opinion, which is great fun, especially with questions like *Which food is the smelliest?!* A variation on the game is to focus on people you know (*Who is the jolliest? Who's the most serious?*). Games like these develop your child's vocabulary and interest in words.

With these activities, eating out not only enables you to avoid cooking but also helps you build literacy in your children.

Diaper Bag Essentials

We all know a diaper bag needs diapers, wipes, and a changing pad. And most of us carry snacks along, too. But supplies to keep hands and minds busy are just as essential. Some supplies are not directly related to literacy, such as a rattle, a teether, or small toys, but others are. Consider packing your diaper bag with the following:

* Favorite books that you rotate regularly

* The current issue of a children's magazine

* Paper and markers for older children

* A magnetic doodle board or other no-mess, nonhazardous writing surfaces

* Stickers, stamps, stationery, and other writing essentials

Literacy on Errands

Dropping off dry cleaning, going shopping, returning library books...
Errands are, for many of us, one of the least favorite parts of life. They
must be done, yet the feeling of accomplishment after completing them
is usually pretty minimal. You can boost that feeling by taking advantage
of the literacy opportunities that errands provide.

Make a List

If you have several errands to run, jot them down on a list or, if your
child is able, have him do it. Attach the list to a clipboard or other hard
surface. Then, as you complete each errand, have your child cross it off
and read you the next one. (If your child can't read it, have him tell you
the first letter or the number of letters so you can "guess" it.)

Talk About the Print You See

Read and explain the words on the ATM machine as you make a with-
drawal, perhaps letting your child press some of the buttons. Point out
the brochures at the travel agency and talk about fun vacation destinations. Make sure your child sees the many forms of print at the post
office—and how they're used. Engaging in simple activities like these
reinforces your child's emerging understanding about the many purposes
of literacy, and helps him to become more sensitive and responsive to
print in the environment.

Go on an Alphabet Hunt

Make a game out of searching for alphabet letters on errands. The game
can vary depending on the child's letter-recognition skills. If your child
has very basic skills, he can look for individual letters randomly (as
opposed to numbers or other shapes). Or, if his skills are more advanced,
he can look for the letter that begins his first name, letters she knows,
or individual letters in alphabetical order. This is also a great driving
activity—hunting for letters on all the license plates, billboards, or road
signs around you.

Making the Most of Common Errands

The following titles are great books for talking about places we might go while running errands. Consider having a book basket in your vehicle for your child as you head out for your more mundane but necessary trips.

Destination:	Book suggestions:	Activity while you're at the destination:
Post Office	**The Post Office Book: Mail and How It Moves** by G. Gibbons **The Post Office** by D. Armentrout	* Before you go, address an envelope to your child and invite him to write a letter to himself. Mail it together. How long did it take to get the letter? * Alternatively, mail a letter to faraway family members inviting them to write back. * Look together at all the different options for stamps. Let your child choose the type to buy.
Grocery Store	**A Trip to the Grocery Store** by J. Keogh **Our Corner Grocery Store** by J. Schwartz	* I Spy is an excellent grocery store game. Try "I spy something yellow" (or that starts with a /b/ sound, or that we eat for breakfast) to help your child start to think in categories or make letter-sound connections.
Library	**Library Lion** by M. Knudson **Homer the Library Cat** by R. Lindbergh	* Children's storytime is a great time to visit the library, but sometimes we go when it's not storytime. Help your child find a good book based on a question that he's asked you that day. * Have a designated "library bag" that you can fill with as many books as your child is old (e.g., four-year-olds can choose four books).
Child Care/ School	**Maisy Goes to Preschool** by L. Cousins **Going to School** by M. Radabaugh	* Pack a note to your child into his backpack. Encourage him to have the teacher read it to him during the day. Ask him to write you back.
Doctor's Office	**My Friend the Doctor** by J. Cole **Going to the Doctor** by A. Civardi	* Bring a book about the human body so your child can look at the parts of the body while you wait. (Try *The Human Body: Lift the Flap and Learn* by P. Hedelin.)

Kjirsten Blander

Erin Hoey Lindstrom

The Grocery Store

For many parents, the most dreaded of all errands is the trip to the grocery store with children in tow. But from a literacy perspective, it is also among the richest in text and language. The next time you visit a grocery store, look around. Print is everywhere—from aisle markers hanging from the ceiling to labels on products and shelves, to the writing on the cakes, to the magazines and coupons at the register, and much more. And because many of the products have familiar colors, designs, and type treatments, even children who do not yet recognize individual letters may recognize the product, and that is a form of "reading." For example, your child may recognize the yellow box of her favorite cereal or the sparkly logo on her favorite toothpaste. So try to think of your next trip to the grocery store not as a chore but as a literacy adventure!

Top: A trip to the grocery store helps children see many uses of print: to label, as on food products and sections of the store; to advertise, as in the weekly circular; to inform, as with nutrition information on the products; to entitle, as with coupons; to remember, as with a shopping list; and more.

Right: After a trip to the grocery store, this child recounted his experience by drawing and dictating to his parent.

I saw a donut. I saw a treat. I saw a chicken. I saw a marker. I saw everything.

Teach New Words

Every errand has some words that go with it. Perhaps the words *stain* or *mend* come up at the dry cleaners; perhaps the words *prescription* or *dosage* come up at the pharmacy. So aim to teach your child one or two new words while carrying out your errands. Then try to provide contexts later for you and your child to use the words again to help cement them into her vocabulary.

Connect to Books

There are many children's books related to common errands. Ask your local librarian or bookseller for books related to an errand you need to run. Read the books to your child before you run an errand or after you've finished, and help him make connections between the book and where you went and what you did there. You'll find this makes the errand feel more like a field trip!

Sharing Children's Books With the Community

Another way to demonstrate the importance of literacy to your child, and at the same time to do something for your community, is to start or volunteer in a program that donates books to a worthy site such as a homeless shelter, community program, or childcare center. You might start a gently used book collection at a local business, school, or church. You might contact Reading Is Fundamental (rif.org) to inquire about starting or volunteering in one of their book-sharing programs. Or you might volunteer in a local bookstore's book-giving program. Many bookstores run one of these during the December holidays (or could start one with your help). The bookstore teams up with a group that works with children who have few books or resources to buy them, such as a family crisis center or social service center. (Your local Salvation Army may help you identify such places.) The group provides a list of the ages, gender, and, when possible, interests of children they work with. A tree or wreath is then decorated with little slips of paper containing this information. Bookstore customers can select a slip of paper and purchase an appropriate book for that child. The bookstore then wraps the books (with help from volunteers like you!) and provides them to the local group to distribute. This can be a wonderful way to involve your child in literacy as well as giving.

Theresa McMannus

Literacy in the Car, on a Bus, on a Train, and on a Plane

The next time you are on public transportation, take a careful look at the children around you. Nine times out of ten, you will find an obvious difference between those who are well behaved and those who are so antsy you're afraid they're going to pull the emergency exit handle for entertainment. Chances are, the well-behaved children have things to occupy them—toys, books, paper, markers, and so forth. And, for at least some of the trip, their parents are using those materials with them. Those who are not so well behaved often have little or nothing to do, and parents who aren't doing much more than reprimanding them for acting up! Nell was once on a four-hour flight with a 3-year-old child whose parent brought nothing for the child to do. And the parent was exasperated that the child kept interrupting her as she tried to read her magazine! (Because of that experience, Nell now carries children's books on many plane trips and passes them out to children when needed, making her sort of a Johnny Appleseed of the skies!)

When you travel, whether by plane, train, bus, or car, plan some activities for your child to do, preferably ones that require materials that promote literacy.

Pen and Paper

Many children can spend a long time entertaining themselves with just a pen and some paper. Some activities, such as passing notes (see Literacy in Restaurants on pages 174–175), playing tic-tac-toe, and making a list, most likely will require your help. But there are lots of activities kids can do without you. Nell's daughter used to fill whole notebooks with scribble-writing, and the big game was to see how many pages she could fill. Drawing pictures, making letters and other symbols, writing "I love Mom" notes—all of these keep little hands and minds busy during travel.

No-Mess Materials

As mentioned earlier, if your little Hemingway has trouble keeping pen on paper, there are some great no-mess alternatives. Magnetic doodle boards, gel boards, and other surfaces allow children to draw and write without any risk of carry-over onto other surfaces. Crayola's Color Wonder® markers—markers that work only on a specific kind of paper and *not* on walls, tray tables, fabric, or elsewhere—are also great for travel. Of course, keeping a supply of wipes handy is never a bad idea!

A Map

If you are traveling any distance, a map is a great tool to have on hand for children. Younger children may enjoy just holding the map or folding and unfolding it—or at least attempting to. Older children may enjoy locating their home and destination and following the route. (You may want to highlight these locales in different colors ahead of time.) Map reading is an important skill you can promote naturally and pleasurably during travel. If you have Internet access, visiting mapquest.com before the trip can be fun to do with your child. You can have her help you figure out what to enter in the fields and then have a map printed out for your use. The printed map will be smaller and have the route drawn right on it, making it easy for little ones to understand.

Books

One of the best ways to prevent your tot from chewing through the seatbelt out of sheer boredom is by doing one of the simplest, most basic things you can do to promote literacy: give him a book. For infants and toddlers, we advise bringing books that allow for movement within their constrained spaces, such as lift-the-flap books, touch-and-feel books, song books, and fingerplay books. For preschoolers, we advise bringing at least a few books that are brand new to the child, as well as a few of his favorites.

You won't be surprised by our suggestion to bring some books related to the trip—for example, a book about airplanes if your trip requires air travel, books related to oceans if you're going on a beach vacation, books about the state you are visiting, and so on. A children's librarian or children's literature specialist at a bookstore should be able to help you locate appropriate titles. Don't shy away from bringing one or two books that seem too long for your child to sit through or too difficult for her to understand. She may enjoy hearing just parts or just looking at the pictures and having you read the captions.

Raymond Coutu

Magazines

For bus and plane travel, magazines are nice because they're lighter than books. They're great for car travel, too, because it's no big deal if they get greased, wrinkled, or otherwise soiled by your little road warrior. There are a number of magazines appropriate for young children (see Chapter 3 for suggestions), which can be ordered online or through a catalog, purchased at a bookstore, or, in some cases, borrowed in laminated form from a local library before your trip.

CDs and DVDs

Many other kinds of media can be taken on car, bus, train, and plane rides. You can bring CDs or downloads of favorite songs and enrich those phonological awareness skills! (See Chapter 5 for more on phonological awareness.) CD or downloadable versions of picture books are another terrific option. Libraries offer a selection of audiobooks on CD or for download. They also may carry Playaway, a small device you can use for listening to pre-loaded audio and video content. The companion book will allow your child to follow along as he listens. And there are good choices for DVDs as well. (See Screen Time on the next page.)

WHILE TRAVELING

Screen Time

You may be wondering about the impact of screen time on your child's literacy development. Here's our take: If you let mindless movies or television shows play continuously without any parental interaction, or if you allow children to spend a lot of time playing video games and using apps that you did not carefully select, then you probably aren't doing your child's language and literacy development any favors. However, video versions of children's books, as well as educational video games, apps, and television programs can be excellent resources, if you engage your children before, during, and after they play or watch. (See Chapter 5 for more information about television, movies, and other electronic media.)

Your Voice and Your Ears

Probably the most important thing you can do in a car, bus, train, or plane is listen and talk to your child. We cringe when we see parents driving by, cell phones at the ear, while children sit miserably in the backseat. And we fear portable DVD players may be the worst thing to happen to family conversation since the TV dinner. The car provides a wonderful context for sustained conversation with your child—so use it! (See Chapter 4 for more about how and why to develop your child's oral language through conversation.)

By taking along these ideas on your next trip, "Are we there yet?" can become "Are we there already?"

Many excellent children's books are available on DVD through bookstores or your local library. Because each selection is only the length of a children's picture book, they work well even for short trips.

Literacy on Vacation

Literacy does not have to start and stop while you're on the road, on the tracks, or in the air. There are ways to incorporate it throughout your vacation. Whether storytelling by the campfire, using a guidebook to find your way around the city, or cuddling up in the hotel bed for a read-aloud, you can incorporate literacy before, during, and after the vacation.

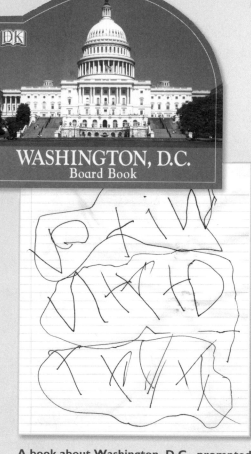

Before: Involve children in planning the trip.

Your child can help you look at websites, consult guidebooks, talk with friends or family members who have been to the destination, and so on. Have your child work with you to build an itinerary or just write a list of a few things she wants to do. Be sure to bring the list along and cross off activities as you do them.

During: Keep a travel log with children.

Each day, write a list of the things you've done, photos you've taken, people you've met, and/or things you've learned. You can buy an official travel journal before your trip, or just use a simple notebook. And if you forget to do that, use the hotel stationery! These notes will be especially useful if you choose to do the "after" activity on the following page. An alternative or addition is to send a series of postcards to friends and family. Children will love picking them out, and friends and family will love getting them!

A book about Washington, D.C., prompted this child to make a list of things she would like to see on her visit there.

continued on the next page

Here is an excerpt from the travel journal of a child visiting the Field Museum in Chicago. The text that accompanies her drawing says, "We went to the Field Museum. We saw the skeleton of a T Rex named Sue."

After: Encourage children to write about the trip.

Work with your child to make a book about your vacation or a topic you learned about while on vacation. He can dictate to you as you write, or write himself with your help in spelling words, forming letters, and getting his ideas down on the page. We've found it helps a lot to have photographs from the trip to help the child remember and describe what he did or learned. And, of course, these photographs can be used to illustrate the book. Your child may also want to include an "About the Author" page, dedication, and copyright page to lend authenticity to his book. He will undoubtedly enjoy sharing his vacation book with friends or family members. In fact, don't be surprised if he becomes so familiar with the book, he can read it to others. If you want to save the book for posterity, consider having it laminated at a local copy shop.

The scrapbooking craze has swept the nation, which means there are many materials available for creating lovely, lavishly decorated books or scrapbook pages about favorite family trips. But remember what the book says is more important than how it looks. Focus on content first, aesthetics second.

Literacy on Day Trips

You don't need to be on vacation to provide lots of opportunities for literacy. The before, during, and after activities suggested on pages 187–188 can be carried out on day trips, too, and there are lots of possible books to go with day trips as well. Remember, good readers make connections between their knowledge and experiences and the texts they are reading.[87] You can help children make these connections as you read aloud destination-related books. See the next page for suggestions.

Raymond Coutu

Even day trips can provide a great deal of exposure to print.

David Ammer

A trip to an ice-cream parlor presents opportunities to read flavor tags and many other texts.

A book about a day trip to an aquarium

Day Trip Book Links

Art Museum

Babar's Museum of Art
by L. de Brunoff

I Spy: An Alphabet in Art
by L. Micklethwait

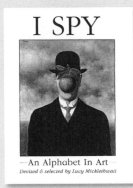

Museum ABC
by The Metropolitan Museum
of Art

Construction Site

Construction Zone
by T. Hoban

**Goodnight, Goodnight
Construction Site**
by S. Rinker

Machines at Work
by B. Barton

Farm

**Farmer Brown Shears His
Sheep: A Yarn About Wool**
by T. Sloat

My First Farm Board Book
by S. Awan

The Year at Maple Hill Farm
by A. and M. Provensen

Orchard

Apples
by G. Gibbons

Picking Apples and Pumpkins
by A. Hutchings

Pumpkin Circle
by G. Levenson

The Shore

At the Beach
by H. Y. Lee

Beach Day
by K. Roosa

Hello Ocean
by P. M. Ryan

**Seagull by the Shore: The
Story of a Herring Gull**
by V. G. Birch

Fire Station

Fire! Fire!
by G. Gibbons

Firefighters A to Z
by C. L. Demarest

Fireman Small
by W. H. Yee

Zoo

A Children's Zoo
by T. Hoban

**Bright Baby Touch and Feel
at the Zoo**
by R. Priddy

Dear Zoo
by R. Campbell

Literacy in the Great Outdoors

Think about sitting down with a good book. Where do you see yourself? At home in your bed? In an easy chair? At the kitchen island, with a freshly brewed mug of coffee? That's fine, but the great outdoors also provides many wonderful places to read, especially for children.

Read Out Loud Outdoors

Consider a hammock, play structure, tent, porch, or balcony for reading aloud to your child or encouraging him to browse favorite books on his own. Or create a reading space by draping an old bedsheet or tarp over a picnic table. Your child will love it!

Marcel Charpentier

Literacy at Places of Worship

Print abounds in many places of worship. Help your child to see and engage with it. You might want to read aloud the bulletin or program before the service begins. Run your finger under lines of text as you sing from a songbook or pray from a prayer book during the service. Bring your child along as you sign up for committees or upcoming activities after the service. At home, read about issues that were raised at the service to help your child better understand them and talk about them. If your child attends childcare or school where you worship, be sure to read together the handouts from her program. In short, use the texts from your place of worship to promote literacy in all environments.

Go on "Book Picnics"

Going on a picnic? As you're packing up the sandwiches, chips, drinks, and cookies, don't forget another essential item: books. Bring along a big blanket, too, and perhaps patio or beach chairs. Big pillows or stuffed animals add a comfy touch. Quite a number of children's books deal with picnics. (Simply search for "picnic" in the children's books database next time you are at the library or bookstore.) You might want to bring some of those books along, as well as some of your favorites on whatever topic your child is passionate about at the moment. Take advantage of a cloudy day by reading *It Looked Like Spilt Milk* by Charles G. Shaw, and then see what you can spy in the clouds. A favorite memory of Susan's daughter is of falling asleep under a big shade tree in the yard while sharing a book with her mom. You'll be building more than literacy in this special, intimate time.

Offer Texts Related to What Your Child Sees Outdoors

From picture books to field guides to nature magazines, many texts for children focus on outdoor experiences. For a few ideas, see Eight Great Books for the Great Outdoors on the following page. After you've finished reading, help your child make connections between the book's topic and her own experience. For example, after collecting insects and other crawly creatures, help your child look up her discoveries in a book on insects. Read the information to your child. Then have her use what she learns to make observations about the creature's appearance and behavior, provide food for it, and return it to its natural habitat.

Paper and writing utensils are also good materials to have outdoors.

Shannon Poynter

Eight Great Books for the Great Outdoors

Infants

Look, Look Outside
by P. Linenthal

Baby Animals of the Woodland Forest
by C. Bredeson

Toddlers

About Birds: A Guide for Children
by C. Sill

Pop! A Book About Bubbles
by K. B. Bradley

We're Going on a Bear Hunt
by M. Rosen

Preschoolers

Insects
by R. Bernard

In the Woods: Who's Been Here?
by L. B. George

Sing a Song of Seasons
Children's Press

Raymond Coutu

There is almost no end of opportunities to connect books with children's outdoor experiences. Does your preschooler enjoy blowing bubbles? Check out *Pop! A Book About Bubbles* by Kimberly Brubaker Bradley, with photographs by the fabulous Margaret Miller.

Get a Move On!

Your child can simultaneously build literacy and burn off some energy by singing and dancing outdoors. Look for songs that build phonological awareness and encourage movement at the same time. For example:

I'm run-ning run-ning run-ning, I'm run-ning run-ning run-ning, I'm run-ning run-ning run-ning, and now I stop!

Jump-rope rhymes also encourage movement and help build literacy. If you need good ones to try, look for collections such as *Anna Banana: 101 Jump Rope Rhymes* by Joanna Cole or for picture books that feature a single rhyme, such as *Miss Mary Mack* by Mary Ann Hoberman. If your child can't jump-rope yet (most under-5s can't), allow him to create his own expressive moves as you recite the rhyme.

David Armistead

Provide Materials for Writing and Drawing

Sidewalk chalk, sidewalk paint, spray foam . . . these materials encourage drawing and writing outdoors, and are relatively easy to clean up. Or you can simply let Mother Nature handle cleanup with a rainstorm.

Another use of sidewalk chalk is to create sidewalk chalk stories. Children draw pictures of all kinds of things, and then an adult gets them started using the pictures to tell a story. For example, you might say, "Once upon a time there was a [hop on castle picture] castle. In the castle, there was a prince. One day, the prince was flown away by a [hop on spaceship picture] spaceship. . . ." The story continues until you've hopped on all the pictures. Children very quickly can start to do their own storytelling from the pictures they draw.

Raymond Coutu

Outdoor painting is a great activity for birthday parties—or anytime.

Place these materials out frequently and encourage your child to use them. Would she like to create something more permanent? Give her a large roll of paper and chalk, paint, and other art supplies. If she draws a road with sidewalk chalk, ask whether the road needs any signs. If she paints a glorious mural, ask whether she would like to sign her name and hang it in her room when it dries.

Alison Billman

David Armistead

Take Literacy Walks

When taking walks with your child, point out print you see and encourage him to do the same. This sends the message that print is all around and provides opportunities to ask questions about it: *What do you think that sign says*? *Why do you think that sign is there*? You can also develop basic skills during literacy walks. For example, if your toddler is working on distinguishing letters from numbers, you might point out the letters in words on a traffic sign and numbers on houses indicating street address. If he is working on developing rhyming skills, you might help him generate words that rhyme with *stop*. If your preschooler is working on figuring out words using guesses about what might make sense and the first letter, you might ask him to guess what a particular sign says. If he is working on figuring out words using context and most or all of the letters, you might help him read the sign.

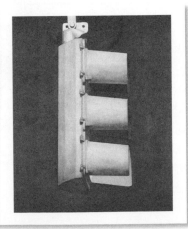

We love Stephen T. Johnson's book *Alphabet City*, in which letters are revealed in familiar city scenes. He has a similar book called *City by Numbers*.

Literacy at the Library and Bookstore

When it comes to venues for supporting literacy beyond the home, the real granddaddies are the library and bookstore. No places more dramatically demonstrate the importance of literacy, or provide more opportunities for high-level literacy interactions, than these two literary meccas, where books are browsed, bought, and borrowed on a continual basis.

The Library

Many families know that making regular visits to the library is important but struggle to work it into their busy lives. One way to do this is to schedule a regular time to visit the library: perhaps every Tuesday evening, after soccer every other week, or on the first Saturday of each month. Then mark your calendar so that you don't forget or double-book, and so you feel more committed to the plan.

Before you arrive at the library, talk with your child about any particular books she is interested in getting—books about a topic of interest or upcoming activity, books by a favorite author or genre (scary stories, counting books), and so on. When you get to the library, give her some time to explore freely and participate in activities the library may be offering that don't involve book borrowing. Some libraries have areas for dramatic play or art projects, for example. And check the library's schedule of events for children's offerings. Chances are, you'll find a regularly

Books About Signs

You might consider investing in one or more books about signs. We like these:

City Signs
by Z. Milich
The only words that appear in this book are in colorful photographs of a great variety of street signs.

I Read Signs
by T. Hoban
This book also features photographs of signs. The book, by award-winning photographer Tana Hoban, begins cleverly with a sign that says, "Come In, We're Open" and ends with one that says, "Sorry, We're Closed."

Take Your Child to Work

If you work outside the home, consider taking your child to work occasionally. And if you don't, ask a family member or friend to do so. All jobs require literacy on some level, and allowing your child to see reading and writing in action sends a strong message about how these activities are used—and required—in society. And you may find your child incorporating things she has seen into her play at home.

David Armistead

scheduled storytime. You might even find visits from local authors and illustrators listed.

Then work with your child to find and select a set number of books and other items to check out (so you don't end up with a pile of 80 books). In fact, to help guide their selection and careful consideration, Susan allows her children to check out the number of books that corresponds to their age—the 4-year-old gets four books, the 5-year-old gets five books, and so on. If you need help finding particular books or categories of books, ask a librarian. That's what she's there for, after all. And you needn't limit selections to books. Most libraries offer books, music, and plays on CD; DVDs of books, movies, and educational television programs; computer programs; magazines; and other forms of media. We feel best when our children leave with a variety of items that excite them. (See Chapter 3 for further discussion of reading materials for children.)

The Bookstore

The bookstore is another favorite haunt of ours. It is a great place for browsing, though you may need to help your child look beyond the books in the rotating display racks (which, unfortunately, are often among the poorest quality) to the high-quality children's literature on the shelves. To give a purpose for browsing, let your child select three books for you to read to him and, when finances allow, offer to let him pick out one book to take home. Look for special events at bookstores, such as children's book readings, author signings, and visits from story characters.

A good way to ensure you visit the bookstore regularly is to rely on it as a place to purchase gifts. We're amazed at how many birthday parties we attend at which not one child gives the birthday boy or girl a book. You may worry that books will not go over as well as toys, but we find this is often not the case, especially because the birthday boy or girl already has the given toy or simply isn't interested in it. Of course, that can be the case with books, too, but the chances are less. Naturally, the excitement around the book depends a lot on the book. For example, many of the turning-5 girls we know would be thrilled with a copy of *Pinkalicious* by Victoria and Elizabeth Kann. Pop-up, scratch-and-sniff, and search-and-find books are also very popular with the preschool set.

Babies generally love books that include photos of other babies, bright colors, or touch-and-feel elements. And many toddlers get excited about books on familiar topics, from going to the farm to using the potty. Whatever your purpose, treat a visit to the bookstore as just that: a treat. And your child will, too!

Concluding Thoughts

We hope that we have helped you to see that the world outside your home is as rich in opportunities for literacy development as the world inside your home. Use the ideas in this chapter to get more out of your out-and-about time—whether you're simply cashing a check or doing something much more exciting and ambitious, like taking a family vacation. In the next chapter, you will learn about how to help make your child's outside-the-home experience literacy-rich even when you're not there—through a collaboration with your child's teachers or childcare providers.

CHAPTER 9

Advocating for Literacy in Your Child's Educational Setting

Kelly Rae Chapin

When we work with parents, we often encounter a whole range of beliefs on the extent to which they should be involved in their children's education. Some parents believe they should maintain a distant or hands-off stance in relation to their child's expert teachers. Other parents think that they know as much (if not more) than the teachers and could run the show themselves. Neither attitude is healthy. Having been, and worked with, practicing teachers, we know that there are few teachers out there who wouldn't welcome parent support. So, how do you find a happy medium? We recommend a "collaboration of experts"—or a dialogue between the people who have a deep understanding of your child, child development, and literacy education— between you and your child's teacher.

You are an expert on your child. There is no one—not his teacher, his doctor, or his neighbor—who knows your child better than you do. You can tell just by looking at him that he's sick. You know when he's feeling frustrated, and you can hear the slightest change in his voice when he's distressed. You know how he learns and what delights him. You are the expert on one.

Your child's teacher, on the other hand, knows about children in groups. (By "teacher" we mean childcare provider, in a center or home setting, or a preschool teacher, in a school setting.) She has specialized knowledge that comes from working with more than one child at a time (or perhaps multiple individual children, over time, as nannies and au pairs do). Many are trained in child development and have more than a few tricks up their sleeve to help children succeed. Your child's teacher is, therefore, an expert, too. She is the expert on many.

Additionally, your child's teacher has access to the expertise of other professionals who may offer support, such as administrators, language specialists, Early Intervention therapists, and social workers.

What we suggest is that the two of you come together as respectful, collaborating partners who honor each other's areas of expertise to advance your child's growth and development when it comes to literacy.

This chapter offers suggestions to maximize your relationship with the professionals who are responsible for your child's literacy development.

You Must Choose, But Choose Wisely

As soon as you make the decision to place your child in someone else's care, you have a whole host of other decisions to make: Do you bring a caregiver into the home—or do you send your child to the caregiver? If you send your child to the caregiver, do you choose a childcare center or a more family-based situation? How many days a week do you send her? Do you choose a program that has children of a mixed or narrow age range? The National Association for the Education of Young Children offers a free checklist of things to think about in choosing the kind of setting that makes sense for your family. It is available in downloadable form at naeyc.org.

Despite the fact that the NAEYC checklist is excellent for thinking about the overall care environment, it doesn't focus on literacy. The Care Environment Literacy Checklist, on the next two pages, is designed to help you assess the literacy-supporting materials and experiences offered in the care environments that you are considering. Recent research reminds us that teacher-child interaction is the most important aspect of a setting though, so weigh these recommendations accordingly.[88]

The Care Environment Literacy Checklist

The items on this list give you a sense of the literacy offerings you might expect to see in a preprimary setting. If you don't see something on this list, don't write off the setting. Instead, ask about it. Ultimately, your decision must be based on a range of your child's needs.

Books in the Room

☐ Books are available at your child's level (picture books for preschoolers, board books for infants, a mix of the two for toddlers).

☐ Adults frequently interact with children and books.

☐ Books are available in a dedicated area for children's independent exploration.

☐ The collection reflects a wide range of types of books reflecting diversity among families and topics (information books, cookbooks, poetry books, guidebooks, storybooks, question-and-answer books, and so on), and other media (magazines, posters, computer programs, and so forth).

Oral Language

☐ When adults are holding babies, they talk and sing with them, make eye contact, and repeat the sounds that babies make.

☐ Adults use language that children can understand yet paraphrase children's language to expand their vocabulary and other aspects of language.

☐ The student-teacher ratio allows for conversation between adults and individual children.

☐ Adults sit with children at snack- and mealtimes to encourage conversation and stretch thinking.

☐ Adults take dictation from children to document their words.

Modeling Literacy

☐ Adults model many uses for reading text.

☐ Adults model many uses for writing.

☐ Adults model a love of literacy.

Literacy in Centers

☐ Writing materials are available at all times for preschoolers and older toddlers.

☐ Adults actively model and engage children in writing experiences.

☐ There is a dedicated area for children to experiment with writing on their own, which includes paper, markers, pens, and so forth. Materials are added and changed regularly to maintain children's interest.

☐ There is no evidence of rote, unsatisfying learning, such as worksheets, flash cards, or other passive activities better left to the later grades.

☐ There is a dedicated area for displaying and investigating interesting natural materials, which is supported by informational books that children can use to learn more about those materials. An adult is often available in this area to advance children's topic-related vocabulary and knowledge.

Continued on next page

Continued from previous page

☐ Dramatic play opportunities are varied and support children's interests. Literacy-related props such as newspapers, appointment books, and order forms are available. Adults join in the play, supporting as needed.

☐ Electronic media are used selectively and with a specific goal or purpose. For example, an iPod may be used to play an audiobook, a tablet may be used to share an e-book, a computer may be used for drawing or writing.

☐ Other centers in the room—such as the block area and art area—also include print.

☐ Adults actively participate in play centers.

Print on Walls and Other Surfaces

☐ Many texts fill the walls, such as lyrics to favorite songs or posters on current topics.

☐ Children's art is displayed with captions and their names.

☐ Cubbies and other storage areas in the room are labeled.

☐ Adults point out and encourage interaction with text.

Read-Alouds

☐ Babies, toddlers, and preschoolers are read to daily.

☐ A variety of text types are read aloud, including stories, informational books, and poetry.

☐ Literacy is included in activities throughout the day—from cooking projects to field trips to circle time.

Using Print for Many Purposes

☐ Print is used for many purposes. For example, a job chart or schedule is posted, and signs are used to alert children to upcoming transitions such as cleanup time.

☐ Preschoolers and toddlers sign in daily.

☐ Outside play includes some text. For example, signs might be used for bike traffic, equipment may be labeled, sidewalk chalk may be available.

☐ Large motor-skills play includes text. For example, signs with arrows that direct traffic or that list the number of children allowed in a particular area are helpful and offer opportunities to use literacy skills.

Credentials or Qualifications

☐ Adults have, or are working on, credentials that include training in literacy and language development.

If you are in doubt about a program, discuss your concerns with the director or teacher. It may be that the activity you were looking for didn't take place on the day you were visiting but typically does. This may be the start of an important relationship, so don't be shy about letting your expectations be known. Ask honest, open questions and listen carefully to the caregiver's responses. Let those in the childcare setting show you what they know as experts in young children's literacy development.

Develop Expert Collaboration

It's important to develop a relationship of mutual respect between you and your child's school setting. Of course the term *relationship* implies responsibilities on both sides. The following suggestions will help you keep up your end of the deal.

School-to-Home Connection

Once you have selected a program, contribute to your child's success. Be as informed as you can be and stay involved by doing the following:

* Read the enrollment information and parent handbook carefully. If your program has a website, read that over carefully as well. (If you did this prior to enrollment to be sure the philosophies are a good fit, reread the information to make sure you truly understand the program.)

* Provide any requested information about your child in a timely fashion (notification of immunizations and allergies, special language you use for eating, bathrooming, and getting along with others, and so forth).

* Routinely read any notes from school, such as newsletters and daily reports.

* Ask questions if something is unclear.

* Carry out suggested home activities to build on what your child is experiencing at school.

* Recognize effective moves the teacher makes and try employing them at home, such as strategies the teacher uses to capture the interest of active children who seem disinclined to listen to a whole book. If your program offers parenting workshops, consider taking them. You will likely learn effective strategies the teacher is using.

* Attend parent meetings such as orientation, parent-teacher organization (PTO) meetings, or family event nights.

* Attend any parent-teacher conferences. (We'll share more about these later in the chapter.)

COLLABORATING WITH CAREGIVERS

* Welcome the teacher to your home if she asks for a home visit. Home visits are rarely home inspections. Although every teacher's purpose is different, for the most part, home visits are designed to give your family the opportunity to get to know the teacher in a comfortable, familiar setting. And, most likely, your child will be delighted to have his teacher all to himself for a short time.

* Honor requests for supplies such as old magazines, junk mail envelopes, or other "beautiful junk," if you can. Children love to bring things from home because it makes them feel they are contributing to their classroom. This also sends your child the message that you think what she does at school is important.

Home-to-School Connection

Communication is a two-way street, so while it's important to take seriously information from the school, it's also important to provide information yourself. What is useful for your child's teacher to know? Here are some possibilities:

* When your child is too ill to attend school, let her teacher know and explain her condition. This shows respect for the school's policies and allows those in charge to alert others to be on the lookout for symptoms.

* If she is not ill, but just "off" because she slept poorly the night before or for some other reason, communicate that as well so that the teacher can be on the lookout for any other behaviors that might give her clues to what's going on.

* If your child is exhibiting some new literacy behaviors at home, such as attempting word-like sounds, turning pages in a book independently, drawing pictures and telling stories about them, or using the letters in her name to label things, pass the information along to the teacher. Teachers are often so busy it takes them a while to catch those exciting milestones. But by calling attention to them, you give the teacher important information she can use to enhance her work with your child.

* Ask if there are ways you can support the teacher's work. Is there anything you can do at home that would make life easier for the teacher, such as setting up field trips or assembling small blank books for the writing center? Could you volunteer in the classroom at times?

* Offer materials. Might you send in magazines for children to use for activities? Do you have two copies of *Curious George*? Contribute one to the school. Is your child's birthday approaching? Celebrate with books or other literacy-related materials instead of gooey treats. Rather than giving the teacher a gift at holidays, consider purchasing a book on your child's behalf as a gift to the school or the program. Have her help you select it. Or consider giving a gift certificate to a local bookstore or online bookstore.

* Develop a healthy relationship with your child's teacher. Be friendly without being nosy. Say hello each time you see her. Make good eye contact and smile . . . let her know you are happy to see her. Ask big questions about the program or small ones about your child's day. Share positive comments that your child makes about school. Invite her to call you at any time with questions or concerns about your child. These overtures send a strong message that you value the teacher's efforts and are willing to do what you can to support them.

* Focus on literacy. Again, though we recommend conversations with the teacher about all aspects of development, don't overlook the literacy component. Ask if your child is talking with other children. Find out what literacy experiences the teacher offers each day. Ask about ways you might support those experiences. Ask if there are materials the teacher needs to enhance those experiences and provide them, as your budget allows. If there is a parent group, mention the need for materials at your next meeting.

What Are the Warning Signs of a Developmental Delay and What Should I Do If I See Them?

This is a tough question in the early years. Some of what you are asking is, "Developmentally, how far off is off?" The guidelines presented in Chapter 2 of this book can help you think about where your child falls in the range. Typically, if you see that your child is falling a year or more behind the expectations, you'll want to have a discussion with his pediatrician to see if there may be any organic reason for the delay (hearing loss, for example, owing to chronic ear infections can significantly delay language development). Together you can decide the next steps to take, if any. In nearly every community, children in the early years can be evaluated for special support services at low or no cost. Typically, these services are offered through the county and are affiliated with the individual school district where your child will be enrolled. Your pediatrician, again, is an excellent starting point in connecting to these services, as is your child's teacher if your child attends any kind of preschool program. The Get Ready to Read website, getreadytoread.org, advises that if you see your preschooler experiencing persistent problems in the following areas, you may want to consult the professionals in your child's life for advice:

* Learning the alphabet

* Rhyming words

* Connecting sounds and letters

* Copying letters and numbers

* Learning new vocabulary

* Retelling stories

* Counting

* Remembering newly learned information

* Paying attention

* Playing with peers

* Moving from one activity to another

* Following directions and routines

Keep in mind that all children have times when they may or may not be interested in certain activities; what you are looking for is a consistent pattern of behavior that may indicate that additional advice is needed.

The Parent-Teacher Conference

The parent-teacher conference. The mere mention of it probably conjures up the image of two or three adults sitting across from one another in tiny chairs, uncomfortable and feeling awkward. But that needn't be the reality.

The intent of a good parent-teacher conference is for all participants to update one another about the child's progress and to share information that will ensure that progress continues. As teachers, we try to avoid surprising parents with unexpected revelations. Instead, we share information throughout the year so that it doesn't all come out in the few precious minutes we have with parents in a conference.

What then, you may ask, is the purpose of a parent-teacher conference? It gives you a chance to review your child's strengths and needs, and set goals. Obviously, as parents, we have little control over the format of the conferences, but we should be prepared for them nonetheless. Before the conference, answer these questions for yourself:

* In what ways has my child grown in his literacy since my last conference?

* In what ways have I supported my child's literacy development since my last conference?

* In what ways do I wish I could better support him?

* What do I need to know to be successful in that support?

* What do I need to know about the program to understand how it supports his emerging skills in reading, writing, speaking, listening, viewing, and visually representing ideas?

My Child Has Some Identified Special Needs. Should I Still Be Doing All This Stuff With Her?

The short answer is yes. Every child can benefit from warm and loving times spent talking, snuggling, reading with a caring parent. Even if your child's needs are more involved, the time spent together around literacy experiences can be positive. Of course, having conversations with your child's teachers and therapists can help you think about how best to meet your child's unique needs in this way. Whatever her disabilities, at the heart of the discussion, there is a child—not a child with disabilities, but simply *a child*—and connecting emotionally with her is among your most important roles as her parent. Literacy experiences can serve as another tool for connection while offering your child new ways to explore the world.

What If I Don't Agree
With My Child's Teacher?

It happens. Sometimes teachers have an old view of literacy. They think that literacy experiences shouldn't happen in the infant, toddler, or preschool years; the children simply aren't ready for them. On the other hand, sometimes teachers think preschool should look like first grade, with a formal curriculum that includes structured lessons and worksheets. If, in spite of the careful research you carried out before selecting the program, you find yourself at odds with the teacher, consider these options:

✴ Have a meeting to discuss your view of emergent literacy. Point to sections of this book that shaped your thinking. Offer to make copies for the teacher. (If the teacher seems interested, you might also suggest our book *Literacy and the Youngest Learner: Best Practices for Educators of Children from Birth to 5.*)

✴ Explore whether there might be impediments to employing more appropriate approaches to literacy. Are there enough materials? Might the teacher need more current information about literacy? More adults in the room? How can you help? Let the program's director know that you would like to see more (or more appropriate) literacy experiences in the classroom. Share the Care Environment Literacy Checklist on pages 203–204 with her. If possible, meet with the director and teacher to establish a dialogue about resources, such as more appropriate books for the classroom, or a wider range of literacy materials. (That way, you won't be perceived as a tattler running from teacher to administrator.) Offer to assist in acquiring resources, if appropriate.

For some early educators, emergent literacy is a new idea. It may take some time for them to access resources and change their practice. Allow them that time. Be sure to comment on positive moves as you observe them, especially if they have a desirable effect on your child. A helpful, upbeat advocate is far more effective than an impatient, pushy one!

Margo Brown

* What milestones should I be looking for in the coming months?

During the conference, share your questions with the teacher, and don't be afraid to ask more questions as they occur to you. This is a time to come together to plan next steps for your child. All of you should leave with goals in mind for your child and a plan in place to help him move toward those goals.

Many parents feel that conferences are a one-shot deal—that they literally have only 15 minutes to discuss their child and that's it—conversation over. Not so. If you ever have concerns or questions related to your child or the program in general, request a meeting. Meetings can take place face to face, by phone, or, if need be, by e-mail. The bottom line is that communicating on behalf of your child will only benefit your child.

Concluding Thoughts

Many researchers have chronicled the link between parent involvement in their children's school and their children's success in school. When you are a parent of a preschool-age child, it is critical to forge strong working relationships with the experts working with your child and to share *your* expertise as well. By nurturing those relationships, your child will benefit not only at school, but also at home and in the world. This is an investment that will have huge returns.

Children's Books Cited

Alborough, J. (2000). *Duck in the truck*. New York: HarperCollins.

Alexander, F. (2004). *How does your salad grow?* New York: Scholastic.

Alexander, M. (2011). *A, you're adorable*. Somerville, MA: Candlewick Press.

Aliki. (1996). *My visit to the aquarium*. New York: HarperTrophy.

Armentrout, D. (2009). *The post office*. Vero Beach, FL: Rourke Pub.

Awan, S. (2000). *My first farm board book*. New York: Dorling Kindersley Publishing.

Barton, B. (1986). *Boats*. New York: HarperCollins.

Barton, B. (1993). *The little red hen*. New York: HarperFestival.

Barton, B. (1997). *Machines at work*. New York: HarperFestival.

Barton, B. (2001). *My car*. New York: Greenwillow Books.

Bemelmans, L. (1939). *Madeline*. New York: Puffin.

Bernard, R. (1999). *Insects*. Des Moines, IA: National Geographic Children's Books.

Birch, V. G. (2011). *Seagull by the shore: The story of a herring gull*. Norwalk, CT: Soundprints.

Bond, F. (1996). *Tumble bumble*. Arden, NC: Front Street Books.

Boynton, S. (1977). *Hippos go berserk!* New York: Simon & Schuster.

Boynton, S. (1984). *Blue hat, green hat*. New York: Simon & Schuster.

Bradley, K. B. (2001). *Pop! A book about bubbles*. New York: HarperTrophy.

Bredeson, C. (2009). *Baby animals of the woodland forest*. Berkeley Heights, NJ: Enslow Publishers.

Bridwell, N. (2003). *Clifford's bathtime*. New York: Scholastic.

Bridwell, N. (1963). *Clifford the big red dog*. New York: Scholastic.

Brown, M. W. (1942). *The runaway bunny*. New York: Harper & Row.

Brown, M. W. (1989). *Big red barn*. New York: HarperCollins.

Bunting, E. (2002). *Girls A to Z*. Honesdale, PA: Boyd Mills Press.

Campbell, R. (1986). *Dear zoo*. New York: Little Simon.

Canizares, S., & Chessen, B. (1998). *Rainforest colors*. New York: Scholastic.

Carle, E. (1984). *The very busy spider*. New York: Philomel Books.

Carle E. (1994). *The very hungry caterpillar*. New York: Philomel Books.

Carle, E. (1997). *From head to toe*. New York: HarperCollins.

Carter, D. A. (1995). *Feely bugs to touch and feel*. New York: Little Simon.

Cerullo, M., & Rotman, J. L. (2000). *The truth about great white sharks*. San Francisco: Chronicle Books.

Children's Press. (2010). *Knees and toes*. New York: Scholastic.

Children's Press. (2010). *Sing a song of seasons (Rookie preschool: learn about nature)*. New York: Scholastic.

Christelow, E. (1989). *Five little monkeys jumping on the bed*. New York: Scholastic.

Civardi, A. (2005). *Going to the doctor*. West Chester, PA: Usborne Books.

Cole J. (1989). *Anna Banana: 101 jump-rope rhymes*. New York: HarperTrophy.

Cole, J. (2005). *My friend the doctor*. New York: HarperCollins.

Cole, J., & Calmenson, S. (1993). *Six sick sheep: 101 tongue twisters*. New York: Scholastic.

Conrad, P. (1989). *Tub people*. New York: HarperCollins.

Cousins, L. (2009). *Maisy goes to preschool*. Somerville: Candlewick Press.

Crews, D. (1978). *Freight train*. New York: Greenwillow Books.

Crews, N. (2004). *The neighborhood Mother Goose*. New York: Greenwillow Books.

Crosbie, M. J., & Rosenthal, S. (1995). *Architecture shapes*. Hoboken, NJ: John Wiley.

De Brunhoff, L. (2003). *Babar's museum of art*. New York: Harry N. Abrams Publishing.

Degen, B. (1994). *Jamberry*. New York: HarperFestival.

Demarest, C. L. (2000). *Firefighters A to Z*. New York: Scholastic.

Denton, K. M. (2004). *A child's treasury of nursery rhymes*. Boston, MA: Kingfisher.

De Paola, T. (1985). *Tomie's little Mother Goose*. New York: G. P. Putnam.

Donaldson, J. (2001). *Room on the broom*. New York: Dial.

DK Publishing. (1997). *My first word board book*. New York: Dorling Kindersley Publishing.

DK Publishing. (1998). *My first A B C board book*. New York: Dorling Kindersley Publishing.

DK Publishing. (2003). *Are lemons blue?* New York: Dorling Kindersley Publishing.

DK Publishing. (2003). *Cats*. London: Dorling Kindersley Publishing.

DK Publishing. (2005). *Dogs*. London: Dorling Kindersley Publishing.

DK Publishing. (2005). *Playtime peekaboo!* New York: Dorling Kindersley Publishing.

DK Publishing. (2004). *Washington, D.C. board book*. New York: DK Publishing.

Dr. Seuss. (1957). *The cat in the hat*. New York: Random House.

Dr. Seuss. (1960). *One fish two fish red fish blue fish*. New York: Random House.

Dr. Seuss. (1963). *Hop on Pop*. New York: Random House.

Dr. Seuss. (1970). *Mr. Brown can moo! Can you? Dr. Seuss's book of wonderful noises*. New York: Random House.

Dr. Seuss. (1974). *There's a wocket in my pocket*. New York: Random House.

Elting, M., & Folsom, M. (1985). *Q is for duck: An alphabet guessing game*. New York: Clarion Books.

Emberley, E. (2001). *The wing on a flea: A book about shapes.* Boston: Little, Brown.

Falwell, C. (1993). *Feast for 10.* New York: Clarion Books.

Fleming, D. (2002). *Alphabet under construction.* New York: Henry Holt & Co.

Foote, B. J. (2001). *Cup cooking: Individual child portion picture recipes.* New York: Gryphon House.

Fourment, T. (2004). *My water comes from the rocky mountains.* Boulder, CO: Roberts Rinehart Publishers.

Freeman, D. (1968). *Corduroy.* New York: Puffin.

Galdone, P. (1972). *The three bears.* New York: Clarion Books.

George, L. B. (1995). *In the woods: Who's been here?* New York: Greenwillow Books.

Gibbons, G. (1982). *The post office book: Mail and how it moves.* New York: HarperCollins.

Gibbons, G. (1987). *Fire! fire!* New York: HarperTrophy.

Gibbons, G. (1991). *Whales.* New York: Holiday House.

Gibbons, G. (2000). *Apples.* New York: Holiday House.

Glaser, L. (1994). *Wonderful worms.* Brookfield, CT: Millbrook Press.

Guarino, D. (1989). *Is your mama a llama?* New York: Scholastic.

Hedelin, P. (2011). *The human body: Lift the flap and learn.* Berkley, CA: Owlkids Books.

Henkes, K. (1993). *Owen.* New York: Greenwillow Books.

Hindley, J. (1999). *Eyes, nose, fingers, and toes.*

Cambridge, MA: Candlewick Press.

Hoban, T. (1983). *I read signs.* New York: Scholastic.

Hoban, T. (1985). *A children's zoo.* New York: Greenwillow Books.

Hoban, T. (1993). *Black on white.* New York: Greenwillow Books.

Hoban, T. (1993). *White on black.* New York: Greenwillow Books.

Hoban, T. (1999). *Construction zone.* New York: Greenwillow Books.

Hoberman, M. A. (1998). *Miss Mary Mack.* Boston: Little, Brown.

Hoberman, M. A. (1997). *The seven silly eaters.* San Diego, CA: Harcourt Brace.

Hort, L. (2000). *The seals on the bus.* New York: Henry Holt.

Hutchings, A. (1994). *Picking apples and pumpkins.* New York: Scholastic.

Intrater, R. G. (1997). *Peek-a-boo!* New York: Scholastic.

J. Paul Getty Museum. (1997). *A is for artist: A Getty Museum alphabet.* Los Angeles: Getty Trust Publications.

Jenkins, S. (1996). *Big and little.* Boston: Houghton Mifflin.

Jenkins, S. (2004). *Actual size.* Boston: Houghton Mifflin.

Jenkins, S., & Page, R. (2003). *What do you do with a tail like this?* Boston: Houghton Mifflin.

Johnson, C. (1955). *Harold and the purple crayon.* New York: Harper & Row.

Johnson, S. T. (1995). *Alphabet city.* New York: Puffin.

Johnson, S. T. (1998). *City by numbers.* New York: Puffin.

Kann, V., & Kann, E. (2006) *Pinkalicious.* New York: HarperCollins

Karmel, A. (2005). *Mom and me cookbook.* New York: Dorling Kindersley.

Katz, K. (2000). *Where is baby's belly button?* New York: Simon & Schuster.

Katz, S. B. (2010). *ABC, baby me!* New York: Robin Convey Books/ Random House.

Keats, E. J. (1962). *The snowy day.* New York: Viking.

Keats, E. J. (1999). *Over in the meadow.* New York: Puffin.

Keogh, J. (2012). *A Trip to the Grocery Store.* New York: The Rosen Publishing Group.

Klutz (Eds.). (1987). *Kids cooking: A very slightly messy manual.* Palo Alto, CA: Klutz.

Knudson, M. (2006). *Library lion.* Cambridge, MA: Candlewick Press.

Kohl, M. F., & Potter, J. (1997). *Cooking art: Easy edible art for young children.* Beltsville, MD: Gryphon House.

Kontis, A. (2006). *Alpha oops! The day Z went first.* Cambridge, MA: Candlewick Press.

Kunhardt, D. (2001). *Pat the bunny.* New York: Golden Books.

Lansky, V. (1986). *Feed me I'm yours: Baby food made easy!* Minnetonka, MN: Meadowbrook Press.

Lee, H.Y. (1998). *At the beach.* New York: Henry Holt and Co.

Leslie, A. (2000). *Do crocodiles moo?* Brooklyn. NY: Handprint Books.

Levenson, G. (1999). *Pumpkin circle.* Berkeley, CA: Tricycle Press.

Lindbergh, R. (2011). *Homer the library cat.* Somerville, MA: Candlewick Press.

Linenthal, P. (2012). *Look, look outside.* New York: Dial Books for Young Readers.

Lionni, L. (1963). *Swimmy.* New York: Knopf.

Llewellyn, C. (1998). *The best book of bugs.* New York: Kingfisher.

Marshall, J. (1997). *Goldilocks and the three bears.* New York: Penguin Putnam.

Martin, B., Jr., & Archambault, J. (1989). *Chicka chicka boom boom.* New York: Simon & Schuster.

McCloskey, R. (1941). *Make way for ducklings.* New York: Viking Press.

Metropolitan Museum of Art. (2002). *Museum ABC.* New York: Little, Brown.

Micklethwait, L. (1992). *I spy: An alphabet in art.* New York: Greenwillow Books.

Micklos, J., Jr. (2001). *Mommy poems.* Honesdale, PA: Boyds Mills Press.

Milich, Z. (2002). *City signs.* Toronto, ON: Kids Can Press.

Miller, D. S. (2003). *Are trees alive?* New York: Walker Books for Young Readers.

Miller, M. (1998). *Baby faces.* New York: Little Simon.

Miller, M. (2000). *Baby food.* New York: Little Simon.

Moreton, D., & Berger, S. (1998). *It's a party.* New York: Scholastic.

Munsch, R. N., & McGraw, S. (1986). *Love you forever.* Buffalo, NY: Firefly Books.

Murphy, J. (1999). *Five minutes' peace*. New York: Putnam Juvenile.

Newcome, Z. (2002). *Head, shoulders, knees, and toes: And other action rhymes*. Cambridge, MA: Candlewick Press.

Numeroff, L. (1998). *If you give a pig a pancake*. New York: HarperCollins

O'Connor, J. (2006). *Fancy Nancy*. New York: HarperCollins.

O'Keefe, S. H. (1989). *One hungry monster: A counting book in rhyme*. Boston: Little, Brown.

Palatini, M. (1995). *Piggie pie*. New York: Clarion Books.

Pallotta, J. (1991). *The underwater alphabet book*. Watertown, MA: Charlesbridge.

Parr, T. (2001). *It's okay to be different*. Boston: Little, Brown.

Parr, T. (2003). *The family book*. New York: Little, Brown.

Parr, T. (2005). *Reading makes you feel good*. Boston: Little, Brown.

Patricelli, L. (2003). *Big little*. Cambridge, MA: Candlewick Press.

Pinkney, S. L. (2002). *A rainbow all around me*. New York: Scholastic.

Polacco, P. (2003). *G is for goat*. New York: Philomel Books.

Portis, A. (2006). *Not a box*. New York: HarperCollins.

Potter, B. (2005). *The tale of Peter Rabbit*. Retrieved from http://www.gutenberg.org/ebooks/14838

Priddy, R. (2006). *Bright baby touch and feel at the zoo*. New York: St. Martin's Press.

Provensen, A., & Provensen, M. (2001). *The year at Maple Hill Farm*. New York: Aladdin Paperbacks.

Radabaugh, M. (2003) *Going to school*. Chicago, IL: Heinemann Library.

Raffi. (1987). *Down by the bay*. New York: Crown.

Rinker, S. (2011). *Goodnight, goodnight construction site*. San Francisco, CA: Chronicle Books.

Rockwell, A. (1993). *Boats*. New York: Puffin.

Roosa, K. (2001). *Beach day*. New York: Clarion Books.

Root, P. (1998). *One duck stuck: A mucky ducky counting book*. Cambridge. MA: Candlewick Press.

Rosen, M. (1989). *We're going on a bear hunt*. New York: Margaret K. McElderry Books.

Rotner, S. & Kreisler, K. (1992). *Nature spy*. New York: Macmillan.

Rovetch, L. (2001). *Ook the book and other silly rhymes*. San Francisco: Chronicle Books.

Royston, A. (1992). *Insects and crawly creatures*. New York: Aladdin Books.

Ryan, P. M. (2001). *Hello ocean*. New York: Scholastic.

Saltzberg, B. (2001). *Baby animal kisses*. San Diego, CA: Red Wagon.

Scholastic. (2008). *Five green and speckled frogs*. New York: Scholastic.

Schwake, S. (2013). *Art lab for little kids: 52 playful projects for preschoolers*. Beverly, MA: Quarry Books.

Schwartz, J. (2009). *Our corner grocery store*. Plattsburgh, NY: Tundra Books of Northern New York.

Seeger, L. V. (2003). *The hidden alphabet*. Brookfield, CT: Roaring Brook Press.

Sendak, M. (1963). *Where the wild things are*. New York: Harper & Row.

Shannon, G. (1996). *Tomorrow's alphabet*. New York: Greenwillow Books.

Shaw, C. G. (1998). *It looked like spilt milk*. New York: HarperTrophy.

Shaw, N. (1997). *Sheep in a shop*. Boston: Houghton Mifflin.

Shulevitz, U. (1986). *The treasure*. New York: Farrar, Straus and Giroux.

Sill, C. (1991). *About birds: A guide for children*. Atlanta, GA: Peachtree.

Silverstein, S. (2005). *Runny babbit: A billy sook*. New York: HarperCollins.

Simmons, J. (2001). *Come along, Daisy!* Boston, MA: Little, Brown and Co.

Sloat, T. (2000). *Farmer Brown shears his sheep: A yarn about wool*. New York: Dorling Kindersley Publishing.

Slobodkina, E. (1975). *Caps for sale*. New York: HarperCollins.

Steig, W. (2000). *Pete's a pizza*. New York: Red Fox Publishing.

Stevenson, R. L. (2005). *Block city*. New York: Simon & Schuster Books for Young Readers.

Stillinger, D. (2004). *The Klutz book of paper airplanes*. Palo Alto, CA: Klutz.

Stone, J. (1971). *The monster at the end of this book*. Racine, WI: Western Publishing.

Sturges, P. (2002). *The little red hen (makes a pizza)*. New York: Puffin.

Taback, S. (2007). *Do you have a tail?* Maplewood, NJ: Blue Apple Books.

Tryon, L. (1994). *Albert's Alphabet*. New York: Aladdin.

Tullet, Hervé. (2011). *Press Here*. San Francisco: Chronicle Books.

Van Allsburg, C. (1987). *The Z was zapped: A play in twenty-six acts*. Boston: Houghton Mifflin.

Van Fleet, M. (1995). *Fuzzy yellow ducklings*. New York: Dial.

Walsh, M. (1997). *Do monkeys tweet?* Boston, MA: Houghton Mifflin Co.

Watt, F. (2001). *That's not my puppy: Its coat is too hairy*. Tulsa, OK: Usborne Publishing, Ltd.

Whiting, S. (2008). *The firefighters*. Cambridge, MA: Candlewick Press.

Willems, M. (2004). *Knuffle Bunny: A cautionary tale*. New York: Hyperion Books for Children.

Wood, A. (1992). *Silly Sally*. San Diego, CA: Harcourt.

Wood, A. (1997). *Piggies*. Orlando, FL: Voyager Books.

Wood, A. (1998). *I'm as quick as a cricket*. Bridgemeed (Swindon), England: Child's Play International.

Yee, H. W. (1996). *Fireman small*. Boston: Houghton Mifflin.

Zelinsky, P. O. (1990). *The wheels on the bus*. New York: Dutton Juvenile.

Endnotes

1   National Council of Teachers of English (NCTE) and International Reading Association (IRA). (1996). *Standards for the English language arts.* Urbana, IL: National Council of Teachers of English.

2   Clay, M. M. (1966). *Emergent reading behaviour.* Unpublished doctoral dissertation, University of Auckland, Auckland, New Zealand.

3   Morphett, M. V., & Washburne, C. (1931). When should children begin to read? *Elementary School Journal, 31, 496–501.*

4   Clay, M. M. (1972). *Reading: The patterning of complex behaviour.* Auckland, New Zealand: Heinemann.

    Teale, W., & Sulzby, E. (1986). *Emergent literacy: Writing and reading.* Norwood, NJ: Ablex.

    Whitehurst, G. J., & Lonigan, C. J. (2001). Emergent literacy: Development from prereaders to readers. In S. B. Neuman & D. K. Dickinson (Eds.), *Handbook of early literacy* (pp. 11–29). New York: Guilford Press.

5   Ferreiro, E., & Teberosky, A. (1982). *Literacy before schooling.* Portsmouth, NH: Heinemann.

    Harste, J. C., Woodward, V. A., & Burke, C. L. (1984). *Language stories & literacy lessons.* Portsmouth, NH: Heinemann.

    Sulzby, E. (1986). Writing and reading: Signs of oral and written language organization in the young child. In W. H. Teale & E. Sulzby (Eds.), *Emergent literacy: Writing and reading* (pp. 50–89). Norwood, NJ: Ablex.

6   Snow, C. E., Burns, M. S., & Griffin, P. (Eds.). (1998). *Preventing reading difficulties in young children.* Washington, DC: National Academy Press.

7   Campbell, F. A., Ramey, C. T., Pungello, E., Sparling, J., & Miller-Johnson, S. (2002). Early childhood education: Young adult outcomes from the Abecedarian project. *Applied Developmental Science, 6, 42–57.*

    Gray, S. W., Ramsey, B. K., & Klaus, R. A. (1982). *From 3 to 20: The early training project.* Baltimore: University Park Press.

    Schweinhart, L. J., Barnes, H. V., & Weikart, D. P. (1993). *Significant benefits: The High/Scope Perry Preschool study through age 27.* (Monographs of the High/Scope Educational Research Foundation, No. 10). Ypsilanti, MI: High/Scope Educational Research Foundation.

8   Senechal, M., & LeFevre, J. (2002). Parental involvement in the development of children's reading skill: A five-year longitudinal study. *Child Development, 73, 445–460.*

    Vivas, E. (1996). Effects of story reading on language. *Language Learning, 46, 189–216.*

    Whitehurst, G. J., Arnold, D. S., Epstein, J. N., Angell, A. L., Smith, M., & Fischel, J. E. (1994). A picture book reading intervention in daycare and home for children from low-income families. *Developmental Psychology, 30, 679–689.*

    Whitehurst, G. J., Epstein, J. N., Angell, A. L., Payne, A. C., Crone, D. A., & Fischell, J. E. (1994). Outcomes of an emergent literacy intervention in Head Start. *Journal of Educational Psychology, 86, 542–555.*

9   Bredekamp, S. & Copple, C. (Eds.). (1997). *Developmentally appropriate practices in early childhood programs.* Washington, DC: NAEYC.

10 National Association for the Education of Young Children, (2009). *Developmentally appropriate practice in early ehildhood programs serving children from birth through age 8: Position statement.* Washington, DC: Author. Available at http://www.naeyc.org/files/naeyc/file/positions/PSDAP.pdf.

11 Burns, M. S., Griffin, P., & Snow, C. E. (Eds.). (1999). *Starting out right: A guide to promoting children's reading success.* Washington, DC: National Academy Press.

12 Office of Head Start, Administration for Children and Families, U.S. Department of Health and Human Services, Head Start Resource Center. (2010). *The Head Start child development and early learning framework: Promoting positive outcomes in early childhood programs serving children 3-5 years old.* Arlington, VA: Author.

13 National Governors Association Center for Best Practices & Council of Chief State School Officers. (2010). *Common Core State Standards for English language arts and literacy in history/social studies, science, and technical subjects.* Washington, DC: Authors.

14 Bennett-Armistead, V. S., Duke, N. K., & Moses, A. M. (2005). *Literacy and the youngest learner: Best practices for educators of children from birth to 5.* New York: Scholastic.

15 Beals, D. E. (2001). Eating and reading: Links between family conversations with preschoolers and later language and literacy. In D. K. Dickinson & P. O. Tabors (Eds.), *Beginning literacy with language: Young children learning at home and school* (pp. 75–92). Baltimore: Paul H. Brookes.

16 Hart, B., and Risley, T. R. (1995). *Meaningful differences in the everyday experience of young Americans.* Baltimore: Paul H. Brookes.

17 Galindo, C., & Sheldon, S. B. (2012). School and home connections and children's kindergarten achievement gains: The mediating role of family involvement. *Early Childhood Research Quarterly, 27, 90–103.*

18 Jacobs, D., & Harvey, N. (2006). Do parents make a difference to children's academic achievement? Differences between parents of higher and lower achieving students. *Educational Studies,* 31(4), 431-448.

19 Ferla, J., Valcke M., & Schuyten, G. (2010). Judgments of self-perceived academic competence and differential impact on students' achievement motivation, learning approach, and academic performance. *European Journal of Psychology in Education,* 25, 519-36.

20 Bus, A.G., van Ijzendoorn, M. H. & Pelligrini, A.D. (1995). Joint book reading makes for success in learning to read: A meta-analysis on intergenerational transmission of literacy. *Review of Educational Research* 65: 1–21.

21 Hart, B., & Risley, R. T. (1995). *Meaningful differences in the everyday experience of young American children.* Baltimore: Paul H. Brookes.

22 Winne, P., & Nesbit, J. (2010). The psychology of academic achievement. *Annual Review of Psychology,* 61, 653-678.

23 Duke, N. K., & Bennett-Armistead, V. S. (2003). *Reading and writing informational text: Research-based practices for the primary grades.* New York: Scholastic.

24 Watanabe, L. M. (2013). Preschoolers' reading and writing of procedural texts. Unpublished manuscript, Michigan State University.

25 National Association for the Education of Young Children (NAEYC). (1996). *Technology and young children—ages 3 through 8: A position statement of the National Association for the Education of Young Children.* Washington, DC: Author.

26 Duke, N. K. (2003). Reading to learn from the very beginning: Information books in early childhood. *Young Children,* 58(2), 14–20.

27 Klutz. (2001). *Klutz kwiz kindergarten launch.* Palo Alto, CA: Author.

28 Reutzel, D. R., & Gali, K. (1998). The art of children's book selection: A labyrinth unexplored. *Reading Psychology,* 19(1), 3–50.

29 Bloodgood, J. W. (1999). What's in a name? Children's name writing and literacy acquisition. *Reading Research Quarterly,* 34, 342–367.

30 NAEYC & The Fred Rogers Center for Early Learning and Children's Media. (2012). T*echnology and interactive media as tools in early childhood programs serving children from birth through age 8. Position statement.* Washington, DC: Author. http://www.naeyc.org/files/naeyc/file/positions/PS_technology_WEB2.pdf.

31 Bus, A. G., Verhallen, M. J. A., & de Jong, M. T. (2009). How onscreen storybooks contribute to early literacy. In A. Bus & S. Neuman (Eds.), *Multimedia and literacy development: Improving achievement for young learners* (pp. 153-167). New York: Routledge.

Shamir, A., & Korat, O. (2009). The educational electronic book as a tool for supporting children's emergent literacy. In A. Bus & S. Neuman (Eds.), *Multimedia and literacy development: Improving achievement for young learners* (pp. 168-181). New York: Routledge.

32 Shamir, A. & Korat, O. (2009).

33 Schuler, C. (2012). *iLearn II: An analysis of the educational category of Apple's app store.* Retrieved from http://www.joanganzcooneycenter.org/wp-content/uploads/2012/01/ilearnii.pdf.

34 Fernald, A., & Simon, T. (1984). Expanded intonation in mothers' speech to newborns. *Developmental Psychology,* 20, 104–113.

McRoberts, G. W., & Best, B. C. (1997). Accommodation in mean f0 during mother-infant and father-infant vocal interactions: A longitudinal case study. *Journal of Child Language,* 24, 719–36.

35 Morrow, L. M. (2005). *Literacy development in the early years: Helping children read and write* (5th ed.). Boston: Allyn and Bacon.

36 Adapted from the American Speech-Language-Hearing Association. (n.d.) How does your child hear and talk? Retrieved from http://www.asha.org/public/speech/development/chart.htm.

37 DeTemple, J. M. (2001). Parents and children reading books together. In D. K. Dickinson & P. O. Tabors (Eds.), *Beginning literacy with language: Young children learning at home and school* (pp. 31–51). Baltimore: Paul H. Brookes.

Dickinson, D. K. (2001). Large-group and free-play times: Conversational settings and supporting language and literacy development. In D. K. Dickinson & P. O. Tabors (Eds.), *Beginning literacy with language: Young children learning at home and school* (pp. 223–255). Baltimore: Paul H. Brookes.

McCartney, K. (1984). Effect of quality of daycare environment on children's language development. *Developmental Psychology,* 20, 224–260.

38 Graves, M. F., & Watts-Taffe, S. M. (2002). The place of word consciousness in a research-based vocabulary program. In A. E. Farstrup and S. J. Samuels (Eds.), *What research has to say about reading instruction* (3rd ed., pp. 140–165). Newark, DE: International Reading Association.

39 Bornstein, M. H. (Ed.). (1989). *Maternal responsiveness: Characteristics and consequences.* San Francisco: Jossey-Bass.

Landry, S. H., Smith, K. E., Miller-Loncar, C. L., & Swank, P. R. (1997). Predicting cognitive-language and social growth curves from early maternal behaviors in children at varying degrees of biological risk. *Developmental Psychology,* 33, 1040–1053.

Tamis-LeMonda, C. S., Bornstein, M. H., & Baumwell, L. (2001). Maternal responsiveness and children's achievement of language milestones. *Child Development, 72,* 748−767.

40 Katz, J. R. (2001). Playing at home: The talk of pretend play. In D. K. Dickinson & P. O. Tabors (Eds.), *Beginning literacy with language: Young children learning at home and school* (pp. 53−73). Baltimore: Paul H. Brookes.

41 Katz, J. R. (2001).

42 McKeown, M. G., & Beck, I. L. (2003). Taking advantage of read-alouds to help children make sense of decontextualized language. In. A. van Kleeck, S. A. Stahl, and E. B. Bauer (Eds.), *On reading books to children: Parents and teachers* (pp. 159−176). Mahwah, NJ: Lawrence J. Erlbaum Associates.

43 Beals, D. E., & Snow, C. E. (1994). "Thunder is when the angels are upstairs bowling": Narratives and explanations at the dinner table. *Journal of Narrative and Life History, 4,* 331−352.

Hart, B., & Risley, T. R. (1995). *Meaningful differences in the everyday experience of young American children.* Baltimore: Paul H. Brookes.

44 Acredolo, L. P., & Goodwyn, S. (1996). *Baby signs: How to talk with your baby before your baby can talk.* Chicago: Contemporary Books.

45 Goodwyn, S. W., & Acredolo, L. P. (1998). Encouraging symbolic gestures: A new perspective on the relationship between gesture and speech. In J. M. Iverson & S. Goldin-Meadow (Eds.), *The nature and functions of gesture in children's communication* (pp. 61−73). San Francisco: Jossey-Bass.

Goodwyn, S. W., Acredolo, L. P., & Brown, C. A. (2000). Impact of symbolic gesturing on early language development. *Journal of Nonverbal Behavior, 24,* 81−103.

Daniels, M. (2001). *Dancing with words: Signing for hearing children's literacy.* Westport, CT: Bergin & Garvey.

46 Acredolo, L. P., & Goodwyn, S. (2002). *Baby signs: How to talk with your baby before your baby can talk.* New York: Contemporary Books.

47 Harste, J. C., Burke, C. L., & Woodward, V. A. (1982). Children's language and world: Initial encounters with print. In J. Langer & M. T. Smith-Burke (Eds.), *Reader meets author/bridging the gap: A psycholinguistic and sociolinguistic perspective* (pp. 105−131). Newark, DE: International Reading Association.

48 Thompson, C. M. (1995). Transforming curriculum in the visual arts. In S. Bredekamp & T. Rosegrant (Eds.), *Reading potentials: Transforming each childhood curriculum and assessment* (Vol. 2, pp. 81−98). Washington, DC: National Association for the Education of Young Children.

49 Kellogg, R. (1969). *Analyzing children's art.* Palo Alto, CA: Mayfield.

50 Lowenfeld, V. (1954). *Your child and his art: A guide for parents.* New York: Macmillan.

51 Malchiodi, C. A. (1998). *Understanding children's drawing.* New York: Guilford Press.

52 Clay, M. M. (1975). *What did I write?* Portsmouth, NH: Heinemann.

Dyson, A. H. (1985). Individual differences in emerging writing. In M. Farr (Ed.), *Advances in writing research: Vol. 1. Children's early writing.* Norwood, NJ: Ablex.

Sulzby, E. (1985). Kindergarteners as writers and readers. In M. Farr (Ed.), *Advances in writing research: Vol. 1. Children's early writing.* Norwood, NJ: Ablex.

53 Sulzby, E. (1985). Children's emergent reading of favorite storybooks: A developmental study. *Reading Research Quarterly, 20,* 458−481.

54 Morrow, L. M. (1993). *Literacy development in the early years: Helping children learn to read and write* (2nd ed.). Boston: Allyn and Bacon.

55 Baghban, M. (1984). *Our daughter learns to read and write.* Newark, DE: International Reading Association.

Bissex, G. (1980). *GNYS at work: A child learns to write and read.* Cambridge, MA: Harvard University Press.

56 Sulbzy, E. (1985). Children's emergent reading of favorite storybooks: A developmental study. *Reading Research Quarterly, 20,* 458−481.

57 Whitehurst, G. J., & Lonigan, C. J. (2001). Emergent literacy: Development from prereaders to readers. In S. B. Neuman & D. K. Dickinson (Eds.), *Handbook of early literacy research* (pp. 11−29). New York: Guilford Press.

58 Neuman, S. B., Copple, C., & Bredekamp, S. (2000). *Learning to read and write: Developmentally appropriate practices for young children.* Washington DC: National Association for the Education of Young Children.

59 Piasta, S. B., Petscher, Y., & Justice, L. M. (2012). How many letters should preschoolers in public programs know? The diagnostic efficiency of various preschool letter-naming benchmarks for predicting first-grade literacy achievement. *Journal of Educational Psychology, 104,* 945-958.

60 National Early Literacy Panel. (2008). *Developing early literacy: Report of the National Early Literacy Panel.* Washington, DC: National Institute for Literacy. Available at http://www.nifl.gov/earlychildhood/ NELP/ NELPreport.html.

61 Melby-Lervåg, M., Lyster, S. A.H., & Hulme, C. (2012). Phonological skills and their role in learning to read: A meta-analytic review. *Psychological bulletin, 138*(2), 322.

62 Anthony, J. L., Lonigan, C. J., Driscoll, K., Phillips, B. M., & Burgess, S. R. (2002). Phonological sensitivity: A quasi-parallel progression of word structure units and cognitive operations. *Reading Research Quarterly, 38,* 470−487.

63 Beals, D. E. (2001). Eating and reading: Links between family conversations with preschoolers and later language and literacy. In D. K. Dickinson & P. O. Tabors (Eds.), *Beginning literacy with language: Young children learning at home and school* (pp. 75–92). Baltimore: Paul H. Brookes.

64 Anderson, D. R., & Hanson, K. G. (2010). From blooming, buzzing confusion to media literacy: The early development of television viewing. *Developmental Review, 30,* 239 – 255.

65 Schmidt, M. E., Haines, J., O'Brien, A., McDonald, J., Price, S., Sherry, B., & Taveras, E. M. (2012). Systematic review of effective strategies for reducing screen time among young children. *Obesity,* 20 (7), 1338-1354.

66 Lapierre, M. A., Piotrowski, J. T., & Linebarger, D. L. (2012). Background television in the homes of US children. *Pediatrics,* 130(5), 839-846.

67 Anderson, D. R., & Pempek, T. A. (2005). Television and very young children. *American Behavioral Scientist,* 48(5), 505-522.

68 Moses, A.M. & Duke, N.K. (2008). Portrayals of print literacy in children's television programming. *Journal of Literacy Research,* 40(3), 251-289.

69 Children's Educational Television Guide. (n.d.). Retrieved from http://www.fcc.gov/guides/childrens-educational-television.

70 Bleakley, A., Jordan, A. B., & Hennessy, M. (2013). The relationship between parents' and children's television viewing. *Pediatrics,* 132(2), e364-e371.

71 Reiser, R. A., Tessmer, M. A., & Phelps, P. C. (1984). Adult-child interaction in children's learning from Sesame Street. *Educational Communication and Technology Journal,* 32, 217–223.

Strouse, G. A., O'Doherty, K., & Troseth, G. L. (2013). Effective coviewing: Preschoolers' learning from video after a dialogic questioning intervention. Developmental Psychology. doi: 10.1037/a0032463. ISSN: 0012-1649. [prepublication copy]

72 Rogow, F. (2002). *The "ABC's" of media literacy: What can pre-schoolers learn?* Retrieved July 1, 2004, from http://www.medialit.org/reading_room/article566.html

73 International Reading Association (IRA) and National Association for the Education of Young Children (NAEYC). (Adopted 1998). *Learning to read and write: Developmentally appropriate practices for young children* [a joint position statement]. Newark, DE, and Washington, DC: Author.

74 Mol, S. E., Bus, A. G., & de Jong, M. T. (2009). Interactive book reading in early education: A tool to stimulate print knowledge as well as oral language. *Review of Educational Research,* 79(2), 979-1007.

75 Justice, L. M., & Ezell, H. K. (2002). Use of storybook reading to increase print awareness in at-risk children. *American Journal of Speech-Language Pathology,* 11(1), 17.

Justice, L. M., McGinty, A. S., Piasta, S. B., Kaderavek, J. N., & Fan, X. (2010). Print-focused read-alouds in preschool classrooms: Intervention effectiveness and moderators of child outcomes. *Language, Speech, and Hearing Services in Schools,* 41, 504-520.

76 Fox, B. J., & Hull, M. A. (2002). *Phonics for the teacher of reading* (8th ed.). Upper Saddle River, NJ: Prentice Hall.

77 Piasta, S. B., Petscher, Y., & Justice, L. M. (2012). How many letters should preschoolers in public programs know? The diagnostic efficiency of various preschool letter-naming benchmarks for predicting first-grade literacy achievement. *Journal of Educational Psychology,* 104, 945-958.

78 Beals, D. E., DeTemple, J. M., & Dickinson, D. K. (1994). Talking and listening that support early literacy development of children from low-income families. In D. K. Dickinson (Ed.), *Bridges to literacy: Children, families, and schools* (pp. 19–40). Cambridge, MA: Blackwell.

DeTemple, J. M., & Snow, C. E. (2003). Learning words from books. In A. Van Kleeck, S. A. Stahl, & E. B. Bauer (Eds.), *On reading books to children: Parents and teachers* (pp. 16–36). Mahwah, NJ: Lawrence J. Erlbaum Associates.

79 Beck, I. L., & McKeown, M. G. (2007). Increasing young low-income children's oral vocabulary repertoires through rich and focused instruction. *Elementary School Journal,* 107, 251–271.

80 Anderson, E., & Guthrie, J. T. (1999, April). *Motivating children to gain conceptual knowledge from text: The combination of science observation and interesting texts.* Paper presented at the annual meeting of the American Educational Research Association, Montreal, Quebec, Canada.

Palincsar, A. S., & Magnusson, S. J. (2000). *The interplay of firsthand and test-based investigations in science education.* Ann Arbor, MI: Center for the Improvement of Early Reading Achievement, University of Michigan.

81 Tharp, R. (1982). The effective instruction of comprehension: Results and description of the Kamehameha Early Education Program. *Reading Research Quarterly,* 17, 503–527.

82 Dickinson, D. K., & Smith, M. W. (1994). Long-term effects of preschool teachers' book readings on low-income children's vocabulary and story comprehension. *Reading Research Quarterly,* 29, 104–122.

83 Neuman, S. B. (1996). Children engaging in storybook reading: The influence of access to print resources, opportunity and parental interaction. *Early Childhood Research Quarterly,* 11, 495–514.

84 Johnson, J. E. (2006). Play development from ages four to eight. In D.P. Fromberg & D. Bergen (Eds.), *Play from birth to twelve: Contexts, perspectives, and meaning* (2nd ed. pp. 13–20). New York: Routledge.

85   Bredekamp, S. (2005). Play and school readiness. *Educational Perspectives,* 1, 18–26.

86   O'Connor, C., & Stagnitti, K. (2011). Play, behavior, language and social skills: The comparison of a play and non-play intervention within a specialist school setting. *Research in Developmental Disabilities,* 32(3), 1205–1211.

87   Duke, N. K., & Pearson, P. D. (2002). Effective practices for developing reading comprehension. In A. E. Farstrup & S. J. Samuels (Eds.), *What research has to say about reading instruction* (3rd ed., pp. 205–242). Newark, DE: International Reading Association.

88   Guo, Y., Justice, L.M., Kaderavek, J.N. & McGinty, A. (2012). The literacy environment of preschool classrooms: Contributions to children's emergent literacy growth. *Journal of Research in Reading,* 35(3), 308-327.

Index

Note: Because of space limitations, only book titles and authors listed in the running text, and not in boxed features, are included in this index. All children's titles are listed in Children's Books cited (page 212).

A

Accomplishments
  of infants and toddlers, 18
  of kindergarteners, 22
  National Association for the Education of Young Children (NAEYC) recommendations for, 18
  of three- to four-year-olds, 19
Aliki, 47
Alliance for a Media Literate America, 125
Alphabet
  activities for, 137–139, 178
  knowledge of, *See* Letter-sound connections
  See also Letters
Alphabet blocks, 66, 155
Alphabet books, 48, 139, 141–142
Alphabet magnets, 52, 97
Alphabet puzzles, 158
Alphabetic principle, 41
American Library Association's Notable Children's Books, 46
Apples to Apples, 103
"Apples and Bananas," 112
Art
  and imagination, 86–87
  literacy through, 86–89
  materials for, 88
  preliterate, 34
  publishing, 88–89
Arthur, 125
Attention span, of children, 132
Authentic literacy
  birthday invitations, 96
  dramatic play, 150–156
  e-mail, 49
  letter writing, 95
  note passing, 175
  ordering food, 174
  reading signs, 170, 196–197
  recipes, 54, 84
Author
  evaluating, 46
  point of view of, 148

B

Babies. *See* Infants
Baby Mugs, 121
Baby signs, 83
Barney, 120
Barton, Byron, 163
Bathroom, literacy in, 162
Bathtub, literacy in the, 163
Bedroom, literacy in the, 128–130
Bemelmans, Ludwig, 17
Berger, Samantha, 61
Between the Lions, 120
Birth to three years, literacy development from, 18
Birthday invitations, 96
Blocks, 156–157
  alphabet, 66, 158
Board books, 48
Boggle Jr., 101
Bond, Felicia, 15
Book clubs, 58
Book picnics, 192
Book reviews, 47
Book swaps, 58
Books
  accessibility of, 62
  alphabet, 48, 139, 140, 141–142
  choosing, 46–47
  for day trips, 189
  donations of, 181, 207
  finding on a budget, 58
  games based on, 102
  as gifts, 58
  handling, 41, 135
  how they work, 41, 135–136
  making connections between, 148
  mass market, 46
  about the outdoors, 192–193
  parts of, 136
  suggested for beginning readers, 61
  suggested for phonological awareness, 115
  suggested for read-alouds, 59
  suggested for world knowledge, 144
  to support pretending, 155
  types of, 48–56
  use while traveling, 182–184
  and vocabulary, 16–17
Bookstores, 46
  bargains at, 58
  frequent buyer clubs at, 58
  and literacy, 197

Boston Globe-Horn Book Award, 46
Bradley, Kimberly Brubaker, 146, 193
Bridwell, Norman, 54, 163
Brown, Margaret Wise, 15, 121
Budget, coping with, 58
Burke, C. L., 13, 14

C

Caldecott Medal, 46
Calmenson, Stephanie, 114
Care environment
  choosing, 202
  connections with, 205–207
  literacy in, 202
  literacy checklist for, 203–204
Carle, Eric, 9, 132
Case, upper and lower, 95
Categories, 102, 168
Charades, 102
CDs, use while traveling, 185
Chalk, sidewalk, 194–195
Chalkboards, 65
Checklists
  care environment literacy, 203–204
  home literacy behavior, 39–40
Children's Technology Review, 49
Closed questions, 81
Cole, Joanna, 114, 194
Color Wonder®, 66, 183
Competitiveness, 103
Comprehension
  importance of, 147
  listening or reading, 42
  read-alouds and, 148
Computer
  software for, 49
  writing by using, 66
Concept books, 48
Concept games, 102
Connections, making, 147, 148
Conventional spelling, 94
Conversations, 76–77
  extended, 83
  while traveling, 186
  See also Talking
Cookbooks, 54,
  for children, 86, 171
Cooking, 54, 171
  by children, 85
  talking while, 84–85
  vocabulary of, 85
Coretta Scott King Award, 46
Count the Beats! game, 106
Craft supplies, 67, 88
Creativity, 86–87
Crews, Nina, 60
Crosbie, Michael J., 157

D

Day trips
  books for, 190
  literacy activities during, 189
Developmental delays, 208
Diaper bags, 177
Dictation, taking, 96
Dining room, 30
Dinner table, 30
Directions, reading, 49
"Down by the Bay," 111
Dramatic play, 150–156
  books to support, 157
  described, 150–151
  for infants, 153
  props and materials for, 154–155
  themes for, 154–155
Drawing
  development of, 90–91
  in restaurants, 174
  and writing, 92–93
Drawing materials, 64–66
  edible, 71
  infant-and-toddler-safe, 71
  for outdoors, 194
Dress-up, 150, 154–155
Dry-erase boards, 65
DVDs
  pros and cons of, 186
  use while traveling, 185

E

E-books, 68
Eebees Adventures, 121
E-mail, 49
Elaborating, 149
Electronic texts, 49
Emergent literacy, 12
Errands, literacy activities during, 178–179
Evaluating, 148
Experience, relating reading to, 148
Experience, Text, Relationship (E-T-R), 145
  with infants, 145
  with preschoolers, 146–147
  with toddlers, 146
Explaining, 148
Extended conversations, 83

F

Factual details, 148
Faery Tale Theatre, 120
The Fairly Odd Parents, 123
Falwell, Cathryn, 176
Family
  communication in, 28–31
  connections with school, 205–206
  demonstrating literacy by, 28

Acknowledgments

This is my fourth time working with Nell and my third with Annie. What a privilege it is to work with each of them. They are brilliant women with such integrity that anything we do together is something to be proud of. At the same time, at some point, each of us has said, "Never again!" Writing a book collectively makes for a richer book, but it is just plain hard to do. We were fortunate in that we were ably assisted by a host of very smart and resourceful colleagues who helped us craft this into what you hold in your hands.

Many images in this book come from a video developed by Nell, Annie, Alison Billman, Shenglan Zhang, and me. Photos and artifacts were contributed by many friends and family members, and we thank them all, particulary Meagan Shedd and Janel Bennett. Many friends helped us write from a parent perspective by offering questions that we tried to answer in the book. Heather Pastori in particular rounded up lots of good questions from friends. Rachel Groenhout ably provided updated citations throughout the book.

We were fortunate again to have the opportunity to work with Ray Coutu, our Scholastic editor. Ray has worked with us across all three books and, amazingly, he remains upbeat and fearless in his dealings with us. Ray's careful attention to detail, his genuine caring that the audience connect with the text, and his uncanny knack for finding a way to write better in fewer words what we drone on about, help our books strike a chord with readers. He is Every Reader. He is a gentle genius. And we are lucky to work with him. This time around we were pleased to also work with Sarah Longhi and Lynne Wilson who provided us wonderful encouragement and support throughout the process.

Ultimately, this is a book about families. Although we can't make a causal link, it seems that each book brings a new child into our lives. During the production of the first edition of this book, Annie and her husband Chris Consolati added Noah to their family, while Nell, her husband David Ammer, and their daughter Julia were joined by Cooper. Those little boys are big boys now! In keeping with tradition, the

Bennett–Armistead family is adopting Justus just in time for the release of this edition. These children, along with my others, Tim, Dawson, Violet, and Ababu, serve as a source of inspiration, motivation, and dedication to all of us. We are so lucky to be entrusted with their well-being, and we know it.

Finally, we thank our husbands, Chris, David, and mine, David Armistead, for understanding crankiness, juggling kids and schedules, reading and rereading passages, and taking that one last picture for the book (again). We love you all. Thank you for helping us help other families to be as fortunate as we are.

V. Susan Bennett–Armistead